T0078081

FOR CRYING
OUT LOUD

FOR CRYING OUT LOUD

The Benefit of Emotional Tears and
The Movies that Bring Them On

Sally Scott Creed, LPC-S, RPT-S

Archway Publishing books may be ordered through booksellers or by contacting:

Archway Publishing
1663 Liberty Drive
Bloomington, IN 47403
www.archwaypublishing.com
844-669-3957

Scripture taken from the American Standard Version of the Bible.

ISBN: 978-1-6657-2313-8 (sc)
ISBN: 978-1-6657-2314-5 (e)

Library of Congress Control Number: 2022908362

Print information available on the last page.

Archway Publishing rev. date: 06/09/2022

Contents

Dedication

This book is dedicated to all the clients and friends who have shared their stories with me and given me the names of the movies in this book. To those who read this, I sincerely hope it helps you find ways to let out your tears. Also, to my family who supports me in all things:

My husband, Don
My daughter, Courtney
My son, Adam
My mom, Mary K.

I love you all.

Acknowledgments

I would like to thank all my friends and colleagues over the years that heard my idea for this book and said they thought it was brilliant and couldn't wait to buy it when it was published. So, I'm holding you all to it! There is sure to be a movie in here that touches your heart.

I would like to thank the Lord for putting this project on my heart back in 1998. I have picked this project up so many times since then; written a few pages, researched a few movies, gathered a few more cry movies from people, then put it back on the shelf. I'm happy that I picked it up for the last time and now it's finally finished. I hope it is a book you can keep nearby for those times when you feel like you'd like to have a good cry and need a little help getting the tears to flow.

Acknowledgments

1

Why is This Book Necessary?

I have been in the counseling field for over thirty years. I work with all ages but specialize in working with young children. When I began working with children, it revolutionized the work I was doing with adults. Children are honest, especially about their emotions. There is no guessing what a child is feeling. All you need to do is look at their faces (and sometimes their actions). They wear their feelings well. And they wear their feelings proudly. If children are happy, you know it. They will have great big smiles, and most of them will jump up and down in excitement. If children have hurt feelings, they will look sad and usually let a tear or two drop down their face. And when children are angry, they will usually act this out in some way (temper tantrums, crying loudly, or throwing toys). But once they grow up, their exuberance dies, and they learn to hold every emotion inside. What happened?

As I've said many times, every one of us was once a child. But the sad truth is that once we become adults, we forget the lessons that children teach us or that we once knew. We stuff our feelings, put on our adult "masks" and go out into the world. The saddest thing to me is that most adults have forgotten how to cry—or they do their best to suppress this, and the only emotion they will allow to surface is anger. Anger is not an emotion that helps us, but it's what we allow to come out no matter what goes on in our day. I believe that expressing emotions through tears is a crucial part of our existence and helps us in not only emotional ways, but also physical ways as well.

Early on in my career, back in the early 1990s, I had an epiphany about the role of tears in our lives. I started doing research and talking with my clients and friends about this. I incorporated what I learned into some of my counseling sessions, and I asked practically every person I met to tell me what their cry movie was. I was the first guinea pig in this experiment. I chose three movies and followed my formula. As far as I can tell, it has worked very well in my life, no matter what tragedies I have gone through. And now I am passing this on to you.

This is not a book for you to sit and read through. It's a resource book to help you learn to take off your emotional mask and become like a child again—fully aware of your feelings and emotions, and able to handle them with panache. So keep reading and find out why your tears are necessary for your health.

2

How to Use This Book

This book is not an educational book about tears and crying. Those books have been written before. Though I do give some information on tears and the benefits of crying, this book is mostly a teaching tool to help you understand:

1. Why tears are necessary
2. Why you need to allow your tears to flow
3. What's the best way to release your tears (my formula)
4. A listing of movies (in categories with date of release, rating, and short description) to help bring on the tears

Once you determine that you do need to cry more regularly, I give you my formula for how to do just that. I use movies as the catalyst for tears. There are other mediums that work for some people (music, for one), but I have chosen movies because of their wide variety and subject matter.

This is also a resource book. If you want to use movies as your catalyst, then you can look in this book for movies that apply to whatever issue or problem you are facing or have faced in your past. Watching these movies should bring you to some emotional catharsis, especially if you follow my formula. While this is by no means an exhaustive list of all the cry movies out there, it is a broad compilation of movies that have been recommended to me during my years of counseling both children and adults. My clients and friends have told me these were their cry movies. What constitutes a cry movie for someone is that there is something within the movie that touches a person's heart and causes them to get emotional, usually from some memory they hold. Every person has a different cry movie, and this book has some great ones. With the many streaming services on the internet, it's easy to pick out a movie and play it whenever you need to watch it.

3

This Thing Called Crying

When I was in graduate school, working on my internship at a psychiatric hospital in Houston, Texas, I had a very wise and observant supervisor. She noticed that I rarely ever cried. It wasn't that I was cold and unfeeling; it was that I thought people who cried were weak. I certainly didn't want people to think I was weak, so I did my best to appear strong and tough. Many supervision sessions with her were spent discussing the importance of tears, especially for someone in the counseling profession. That started me thinking about this thing called crying. How could the ability to cry help me in my counseling career? Why was crying so important?

I began observing people both in person and on television. There are some I found who reminded me of Hawkeye Pierce, a character from the hit TV series M*A*S*H* played by Alan Alda. If you ever watched the show, he was the one who was always pulling practical jokes on everyone, yet he couldn't take it if any jokes were pulled on him; he would get very angry. He kept his emotions well hidden, and he used his sense of humor as a defense mechanism. It was rare to ever see him cry. Many people are like this—they keep their emotions hidden and use other methods to release the feelings they have. Some are extremely rude and hateful to others, and some are jokesters—the life of the party. Some are quiet and reserved, and some appear happy all the time (only on the outside). But they have one common trait: they don't readily cry.

In the movie *The Kid*, Bruce Willis plays a highly successful and wealthy image consultant (Russ Duritz) who is also a jerk. He is very cold, uncaring, and unfeeling. He also has a twitch he gets in his eye whenever he is under great stress. He admits that he hasn't cried since he was eight years old. Then he gets a visit from his eight-year-old self, and he believes he's supposed to help the kid through some type of problem. However, he soon realizes that the kid has come to help him. By watching himself at age eight relive a traumatic incident, the grown Russ gets in touch with the kid inside him and is able to cry as a result and thus become more human again. If you haven't seen this movie, it's a definite must-see. It's also one of my favorite movies because I feel like it's my job on film. I help adults revisit their painful memories of childhood and look back at these events with grownup eyes. Then they are able to forgive not only themselves, but also the people who have hurt them. They can release their pain through their tears and finally find healing again.

In the years I have been counseling, I have come to believe that the ability to cry emotional tears is not only what makes us human but it's also what keeps us sane. So many people hold their feelings inside and are afraid to reveal their true selves. Letting out tears is a great way to release hurt, sadness, or any intense feelings we have and help us stay balanced. Tears have also been known to reduce aggression and help us bond with others. I remember when my late husband and I had to put one of our dogs to sleep. He started crying, and it was the first time I had seen him cry. It helped me feel emotionally close to him because I was able to see him as a vulnerable human.

4

How Crying Helps Us

In his book *Crying: The Mystery of Tears* author William Frey explains why humans cry and lists the benefits of tears (Frey 1977):

> We cry at weddings and graduations. We cry at the miracle of birth. We cry when someone expresses sincere appreciation and love for us. We cry when we receive an especially thoughtful gift.

> In the course of a lifetime, humans instinctively weep for a multitude of reasons. It's a rare person who never sheds tears of sorrow, joy, anguish, or ecstasy. Throughout the history of humankind, tears have been intertwined with the very essence of the human heart, for the ability to shed emotional tears—psychogenic lacrimation—seems to be one of the few physiological processes which separates humans from other animals.

> Both animals and humans constantly produce a fluid called "basal" or "continuous" tears, which keeps the surface of the eye moist and helps prevent infection. With each blink

of the eyelid a tear film bathes the surface of the eye with a bacteria-fighting fluid secreted by the main lacrimal gland and by accessory lacrimal glands located in the eyelids. And when the surface of the eye is irritated, the main lacrimal gland in humans and a similar gland in other animals produce additional tears, called "reflex" or "irritant" tears. Anyone who has chopped onions is familiar with irritant tears, which dilute and flush away the strong onion vapors. When a foreign object such as a loose eyelash or grain of sand gets in our eyes, these tears help wash away the irritating invaders. Our body also produces irritant tears when our eyes are exposed to severe cold, dust, or smoke to lessen the harmful effects on the eyes. The extra tears that wash away or reduce the effects of an irritant not only protect the surface of the cornea but also help restore normal vision as soon as possible.

Dr. Frey did a study on two types of tears. One type is called irritant tears—the kind you have automatically when something gets in your eye. The other type of tears is called emotional tears—the ones you shed when you are sad and experiencing deep emotions. His conclusions from this study were that the lacrimal glands do excrete different types of tears in response to different stimuli, and that in spite of the greater volume of emotional tears, they have a higher concentration of protein than irritant tears (Frey 1985).

Something truly unique happens when we shed emotional tears. The reason people feel better after crying is that they may be removing chemicals that build up in their bodies during emotional stress. One substance found in tears is manganese, a mineral that has been implicated in mood alterations. Manganese is thirty times greater in tears than in blood serum. It has also been suggested that suppressing our tears could cause us to feel physically and emotionally worse (Levoy 1988).

Tears are not just the product of emotional sadness and grief. They also play a very important part in keeping our eyes healthy. Our tears contain a chemical called lysozyme, which is an antibacterial enzyme. This enzyme was first discovered in 1922 by Alexander Fleming. Lysozyme was dubbed the "first antibiotic." This enzyme prevents dehydration of the mucous membranes and wards off upper respiratory infections. It has been effective in killing off 90-95 percent of all bacteria in the eye in just ten minutes (Frey 1985).

Cutting an onion often causes tears to flow. Onions release a chemical that turns into sulfuric acid when it comes into contact with the surface of the eyes and could cause great harm if we didn't have tears. Tears basically render the sulfuric acid harmless. Though we hate to cut onions because they make us cry, we can now understand that our tears are a blessing and a great help toward healthy eyes (Frey 1985).

In a study at the University of Pittsburgh School of Nursing, psychiatric nurse Margaret Crepeau found that healthy people are more likely to cry and have a positive attitude toward tears than those (who refuse to cry) with ulcers and colitis, two conditions thought to be stress related (Levoy 1988).

In the years that I've been counseling, I have noticed that some of the meanest and angriest clients I have encountered admitted that they rarely or never cry. Their belief was that crying was for sissies, which, as we now know, is totally false.

5

What's So Great about Tears?

As I have counseled adults over the years, I have asked both men and women about their crying habits. Many of them admit that they are not comfortable crying. One of the fun things I like to do, especially with men, is to ask them to look in a mirror (I have a hand mirror in my desk drawer for this purpose). I have them place their finger near the inside corner of their eye and pull down. Then I ask if they can see a very tiny hole on their lower lid, near their nose. Once they see it, I ask them if they know what this is. Often, they respond that they don't know what it is. So, I let them know that this is their tear (lacrimal) duct. I have them check to make sure they have one in their other eye as well. I inform them that God gave each person two of these. If He had not wanted men to cry, He would have given them only one or no tear ducts. Then I educate them on why tears are important and how they help us heal from our emotional wounds.

Tears have been known to remove toxins from the body, reduce symptoms of stress and help the body heal (as stated in the last chapter). When people are able to cry easily, they are said to be in touch with their feelings. This is a good thing. According to Biebel, Dill, and Dill (2008):

> Tears are not just drops of saltwater, but are alive with hormones, enzymes, and toxins. Tears have critical functions for us, which are:
>
> 1. They lubricate the eyeball and prevent "dry eye."
> 2. They bathe the eyes in Lysozyme, one of the most effective antibacterial and antiviral agents known. Without it, eye infections would soon cause most victims to go blind.
> 3. After crying, people actually do feel better, both physically and psychologically, while suppressing tears makes them feel worse.
> 4. Emotional tears remove toxic substances from the body.
> 5. It is a primary way for the body to eliminate harmful stress hormones, which have been shown to cause serious damage to brain cells. These stress hormones attack the brain sites that have to do with mood disorders.
> 6. They make us more human and give us the ability to connect with others. As Hubert Humphrey once said, "A man without tears is a man without a heart."

Dr. W. Dewi Rees wrote about bereavement saying that men who are bereaved have a higher mortality rate than women, probably because they repress their feelings of grief, and women more readily express their grief. So it seems that widowed men would live longer if they allowed themselves to cry more (Rees 1972).

When I was fifty and my husband was fifty-two, he became very sick. On December first, he was admitted to the hospital and for over a week the doctors couldn't figure out what was wrong with him. They finally did an endoscopy and saw some type of mass in his stomach—so on December tenth, they opted to do surgery to figure out what it was. They found out that it was cancer and they had to remove his stomach and most of his esophagus. Needless to say, he was dying and there was nothing else they could do for him. My daughter was away at college for her freshman semester and my son was at home in his freshman year of high school. As we visited their dad throughout the month of December, it was clear that he wasn't going to recover. He lost his ability to talk, so we made an alphabet board to help him. I was being strong for my kids and for my clients (I still worked during the day throughout all of this). It was 2008 and the movie *Marley and Me* had just come out for Christmas. My kids wanted to see it, so I agreed to go. Even though I love dogs, I thought to myself as the movie began that this was not a good dog and that I wasn't going to like him—which meant that no matter what happened in the movie, I was NOT going to cry. For those of you who have seen this movie, it is a tearjerker. I couldn't help it—I broke down and shed LOTS of tears in this movie. It helped me make it through the next week, because my husband died four days later and I had to remain strong for my kids.

About a year after my husband died, I thought I was handling things well. My counseling business was thriving, and my kids seemed to be doing fairly well, all things considered. A friend of mine loaned me the movie *Love Comes Softly* starring Katherine Heigl. I watched it alone one night not knowing anything about it. That movie is what helped me release all the grief I had been holding in for a year. I cried ugly tears that night and slept like a baby.

All this to say—I have learned to practice what I preach. I cannot stress enough the importance of emotional health. As someone who has made a career out of helping people regain their emotional health, I have learned the importance of crying it out when I get overwhelmed by life or my job. I have often been asked how I am able to do what I do, because most people cannot imagine sitting and listening to people pour out their problems day after day. However, I feel that my job is a calling on my life, and I love what I do. But I admit that I could not be effective if I didn't make sure that my own emotional health was guarded and well cared for.

6

Why People Find It Difficult to Cry

I've had the idea for this book for over thirty years, which is as long as I've been counseling people. As a counselor, I always knew when someone was getting to the root of their problem—at the very moment the tears would start to flow. I also felt very privileged to witness these tears because it meant the person felt safe enough to let themselves be vulnerable and cry in front of me. It wasn't just women who cried, but men as well. One thing we humans have in common is that we all have the ability to cry, whether or not we choose to use this ability.

In our society, it is more readily acceptable for people to have any emotion other than sadness. Go down the list of emotions: angry, happy, jealous, fearful, cautious—pick one. Any of them are more acceptable than sadness. Ask someone who's suffered a loss of any kind. They will tell you that most people are extremely uncomfortable with tears. We don't know what to say or how to react to someone who's crying. I've heard from so many people that their friends don't know what to say to them or what to do when they express sadness, so they just stop showing this emotion to anyone.

It's interesting that out of all the living creatures on the earth, we humans are the only ones who can cry. In spite of this, we don't have any idea how to handle tears. It's the one thing that we work hard to avoid. Yet it's also the one thing that helps us keep our sanity and maintain our humanness.

I've coached many people on what to do to help someone who is sad or grieving. In graduate school, I remember someone telling me to always make sure to have tissues on hand in my office, but to NEVER hand a tissue to a client who was crying. When people are dealing with sadness and their tears are flowing, the worst thing you can do is hand them a tissue. This gives the message that you want them to dry their eyes. What comforts a grieving person the most is that you are there with them. That's it. There are no magical words to say to them, so stop fretting about this. Just sit there. If you feel compelled, give them a hug or touch them on the back or somewhere non-threatening just to let them know you are there with them.

A great movie came out a few years ago called *Inside Out*. It's a Pixar movie about a girl named Riley. Her family moves to a different city away from all her friends. Riley has a slew of emotions in her brain—her "Control Center"—and the movie shows all of them as the ones who are running the show. At first, Joy was the emotion in control, and she managed to keep Riley a very happy child. But once the family moved to a different city, Riley experienced Sadness that turned into Anger because she had to leave all her friends behind. Anger took control to the point where Riley started to run away from home in order to be with her friends. What I found very interesting was that in order to get Anger out of the way, Sadness had to show up first before Joy could arrive again. This is the way it is for all of us. First, we need to express the sadness (through our tears), before we will be able to experience all the other wonderful emotions we have inside.

Another takeaway from this movie that has helped me in my work as a counselor is the use of the characters from the movie. I purchased the figurines and use the main characters (Joy, Sadness, Anger, Fear, and Disgust) as I ask children and adults to line them up in order of appearance in their brain and in their lives. (The one thing I do differently is that I do not use the Disgust character as it is named, but I changed the name to Guilt, since most people deal with guilt more than they do disgust.) It's not only a great way to have them visualize which emotions are being allowed to control their lives, but it's also a great teaching tool to help them remember the important role that sadness plays in helping us find our joy again.

7

What the Bible Says about Tears

The Bible (ASV) says we were created by God (Gen. 1:27) and that we were "fearfully and wonderfully made" (Psalms 139:14). God's design of our human tears is something we don't often think about but is very amazing.

The Bible mentions tears multiple times, proving that our tears are important to God.

In the thirty-eighth chapter of Isaiah, King Hezekiah became mortally ill and was told that he was going to die. In response, he prayed a prayer in which he turned his face to the wall and "wept sore" (Is. 38:3). As a result, God told him that "I have heard thy prayer, I have seen thy tears: behold, I will add unto thy days fifteen years" (Is. 38:5).

When David was overwhelmed before being taken to the Philistine King Achish of Gath, thinking Achish would kill him, he prayed to God: "What time I am afraid, I will put my trust in thee. In God

(I will praise his word), In God have I put my trust, I will not be afraid; What can flesh do unto me" (Psalm 56:3-4)? Then David says, "Thou numberest my wanderings: Put Thou my tears into Thy bottle; Are they not in Thy book" (Psalm 56:8)?

King David cried out to God many times. Being anointed as a young boy (fifteen years old) by Samuel the prophet and being told he would be the next King of Israel, he had to wait fifteen years before becoming King. In the meantime, he was pursued by King Saul, who was very jealous and was constantly trying to kill him. David poured out his heart to God through his Psalms. One time when he was weary, He told God, "I am weary with my groaning; Every night I make my bed to swim; I water my couch with my tears" (Psalm 6:6). Then with confidence and faith, he says, "For Jehovah hath heard the voice of my weeping. Jehovah hath heard my supplication; Jehovah will receive my prayer" (Psalm 6:8b-9). Another time he said, "The righteous cried, and Jehovah heard, and delivered them out of all their troubles" (Psalm 34:17).

Job said in the midst of his suffering, "My friends scoff at me: But mine eye poureth out tears unto God" (Job 16:20).

Jeremiah, known as the weeping prophet, made frequent references to his eyes running down with tears. When God told Jeremiah that He would destroy the people because they had not listened to Him, Jeremiah was deeply grieved. He said to the people, "But if ye will not hear it, my soul shall weep in secret for your pride; and mine eye shall weep sore, and run down with tears, because Jehovah's flock is taken captive" (Jer. 13:17). In the next chapter, God tells Jeremiah that all the prophets were lying to the people regarding the famine and disaster that was to come (prophets told them it would never happen, and they would have peace). God told Jeremiah to say to the people, "Let mine eyes run down with tears night and day, and let them not cease" (Jer. 14:17a).

A sinful woman, when encountering Jesus, showed her faith in Him by her actions. "And behold, a woman who was in the city, a sinner; and when she knew that He was sitting at meat (having dinner) in the Pharisee's house, she brought an alabaster cruse (vial) of ointment, and standing behind at His feet, weeping, she began to wet His feet with her tears, and wiped them with the hair of her head, and kissed His feet, and anointed them with the ointment" (Luke 7:37-38). "As a result of this act of love, Jesus forgave her sins" (Luke 7:47).

At the tomb of Lazarus, Jesus' great friend, "Jesus wept" (John 11:35).

Christ Himself offered up prayers mixed with tears: "having offered up prayers and supplications with strong crying and tears unto Him that was able to save Him from death and having been heard for His godly fear" (Hebrews 5:7).

Tears were associated with Paul's service for God: "And when they were come to him, he said unto them, Ye yourselves know from the first day that I set foot in Asia, after what manner I was with you all the time, serving the Lord with all lowliness of mind, and with tears, and with trials which befell me by the plots of the Jews" (Acts 20:18-19). Then later, "Wherefore watch ye, remembering that by the space of three years I ceased not to admonish every one night and day with tears" (Acts 20:31).

And in the end, some happy news: "And I heard a great voice out of the throne saying, Behold, the tabernacle of God is with men, and he shall dwell with them, and they shall be his peoples, and God himself shall be with them, *and be* their God: and he shall wipe away every tear from their eyes; and death shall be no more; neither shall there be mourning, nor crying, nor pain, any more: the first things are passed away" (Rev. 21:3-4).

All this to say, God created tears for our benefit—to help heal our eyes from irritants, and to help heal our souls from sadness and grief. So when you need to, let your tears flow.

8

What Children Teach Us about Crying

Believe it or not, we were all children once. Some adults seem to have forgotten this fact. In my work, I am considered a child expert. I am a Registered Play Therapist and I work with children as young as two years old. Children do not sit on a couch and pour out their problems to me the way adults do. Instead, they play in a special playroom equipped with carefully chosen toys. By observing their play and verbally tracking what they do in the playroom, I am usually able to tell what they are feeling.

When children experience sadness or pain, they automatically cry. This is a reaction they were born with. As children get older, they are taught to stop crying—either by the adults in their lives or older children. Some children get labeled "crybaby" whenever they cry, and they know that this is not a good thing to be called. These children grow up and eventually do stop crying. The problem is that they never start it up again.

One pivotal question I often ask in a counseling session when I'm working with teenagers and adults is this: "When was the last time you had a good cry?" I am usually shocked by the answers I get. I've come to realize that the angrier and more bitter the client is, the longer it's been since they had a good cry. My conclusion over the past thirty years is that people who constantly avoid sadness, hurt, and pain and refuse to let themselves cry end up very bitter and angry people. Once they learn to express their pain and release the tears, they usually experience a catharsis of sorts and feel a huge release of emotion. Their demeanor becomes softer and more human.

Back in my early years of counseling, I had a young adult male who had come to me initially with relationship problems—then again, when the relationship ended. He didn't have any family nearby, but he had his black Labrador Retriever who had been with him for ten years and whom he loved dearly. He talked about how this dog had helped to cheer him up and was great company. Then one day months later, he came in and said that his dog had died. I was so sad to hear this. I asked him what he was going to do, and he replied that he planned to go out and get drunk that night. I asked him to do me a favor. He was curious as to what I would ask him to do, so he reluctantly agreed.

I told him to first contact his friends and family to let them know he was doing okay once he got home. Then I told him to turn off his TV, radio, phone, and anything that could interrupt him. I asked him to get out all the pictures of his dog and all of his dog's toys, leashes, etc. Then I told him that his dog needed him to grieve his loss because of how special this dog was to him. I asked him to sit home and cry that evening. I actually didn't think he would do this. But I got a call from him the next morning, and he thanked me for asking him to do this. He said he cried and cried and felt so much better because of it. He had released much of his pain and anger, and he could function the next day at work and feel positive and hopeful again.

9

How to Know If You Need to Cry

How can you tell if you're ready for a good cry? What are the warning signs? In a nutshell, you will know. Anger outbursts are a good indicator that you're holding in too many emotions and in need of a release. Your anger will come out of nowhere. Your days are peppered with moodiness and mostly anger. You find fault in almost everyone around you. Your relationships, if you still have them, are suffering. Feeling overwhelmed by situations in your day can cause added stress and tension. You never take time to be alone. You constantly have something around to entertain you (TV, internet, alcohol, etc.). You don't enjoy being alone with your thoughts. You rarely let yourself think of past hurtful events. Also, crying over the slightest thing is another indicator that you need to "dump" those feelings by planning a good cry.

Years ago, when my kids were small, my late husband, when realizing that I was getting increasingly moody and difficult to live with, used to ask me, "Hey, when are you going to watch *Steel Magnolias* again?" This was his cue to let me know that I needed to go have a good cry. Because my job was stressful and my life was busy, I often didn't have time to cry. Usually about every three months, I would schedule time late on a Friday night to watch a cry movie. Without fail, once I had a good cry, I was back to myself again and ready to be positive once more.

10

How to Cry—My Tried-and-True Formula

Maybe you are finally convinced about the importance of crying emotional tears, but how do you make yourself cry? Many clients have told me that they can't just bring on the tears whenever they want. They find it very difficult to cry sometimes. So I've asked them to name a movie that they have seen that made them cry. I've been keeping track of all the movies that were listed over the years, and I've compiled them in this book for others to benefit from. Interestingly, just because a movie makes one person cry doesn't mean that movie will work in eliciting tears in another person. When a movie touches a person's heart enough to elicit tears, it is touching something very deep and spiritual in that person. This is usually the core or main issue that person is dealing with in life.

Finally, how can you use this book? Here's my recommended formula:

First—try to think of a movie you've seen that made you cry, then try to find that movie to watch. These are movies that you've seen once and refuse to watch again because you cried the first time you watched it. Chances are it is listed in this book. I have tried my best to use categories to describe movies (Grief and Loss, Tragedy and Trauma, etc.). If not, search this book for a similar movie with the same or similar subject matter. If you are dealing with abandonment issues, for example, browse through the movies listed in that section.

Second—plan a time you can watch it alone. I always recommend that people watch their cry movies alone. If you watch a cry movie with another person, they may snicker at you for crying or laugh at you, thus killing any attempts for you to "let go" of your emotions. Even if they are completely quiet during the movie, you will still be aware that there is another person in the room, and you will not allow yourself to cry as hard as you would if you were alone. Trust me on this—you don't want anyone around when you are crying!

Third—make sure you will not be interrupted. I often suggest watching a cry movie late at night after everyone in your home has gone to bed. Turn off your electronic devices (cell phones) so you won't be bothered or interrupted. Make sure you are watching the movie without any commercial interruptions—playing a DVD or renting/purchasing a movie online works best because there are no commercials. Commercials will kill your attempts to allow tears, because you may not know when a commercial will pop up and it may be just before the emotionally sad part of the movie. Commercials are taboo when watching cry movies. Then, watch the movie as you normally would.

Fourth—PAUSE the movie when it gets to the part where you feel your emotions start to bubble up from deep within you. Don't stop it or let it continue playing—pause it. This will guarantee that there are no further distractions to break the mood.

Fifth—go ahead and cry your eyes out if you can once the movie is paused. It may help to cry into a pillow if you need to muffle the sound. Initially, you will be crying about whatever you just watched on the movie, but eventually you will continue crying for whatever pain your heart is dealing with.

Sixth—I recommend crying for at least five to twenty minutes. Try not to cry for more than twenty minutes. Some people are afraid that if they start crying, they won't be able to stop. Others think that a couple of tears indicates a good cry. I advise that a five-to-twenty-minute sob is adequate to release the pent-up emotions inside.

Once you feel you've cried enough, either finish watching the movie or turn it off. If it's during the day, prepare yourself a cold glass of tea or lemonade or something refreshing. If it's at night, do your best to try to sleep. You will undoubtedly feel exhausted from the emotional cry, but you will eventually feel calmer and happier. If you watch the movie late at night, your crying will cause you to want to sleep afterward (hopefully).

My favorite time to watch a cry movie is late at night on Fridays. The others in my home are usually asleep, and my phone is set to "do not disturb." It's all MY time, and I can cry as much as I need. I also make sure I have nothing scheduled the next day because my eyes stay puffy awhile, and I need to wait until I look normal again before venturing out. I like to call it a "good cry" because it is good for your emotional and physical health.

So that's the formula. I don't use this very often now. When my kids were smaller, it was about once every 3 months. Now, it's probably twice a year that I feel the need for an emotional release.

My top three cry movies are:

Steel Magnolias—This is my all-time favorite movie (it runs a close race with It's a Wonderful Life)! I have the dialogue memorized because I've watched it so many times over the years. The saddest part of this movie comes just before the funniest part—so if I don't hit the pause button quick enough, I end up laughing instead of crying.

Imitation of Life—This is a movie I usually can only watch once every five or ten years, because it has me crying so hard at the end that I don't need to cry much after that.

Black Beauty—I start crying at the opening of this one because I can't stand to see an animal suffer. It has a fantastic ending that still causes tears, but they are happy tears then.

So now that you have my formula, turn the page for the categories and movie lists. There are some wonderful movies listed here. I hope you find your emotional release in many of them and that you begin to feel "back to yourself" soon.

Happy crying!!

11

Movies

One important thing to look for when choosing a cry movie is to find one that touches the secret and deep places of your heart. If you know what your heart is holding on to, then you will find it easier to choose a movie that touches your heart. Most people instinctively know what their cry movies are, just by watching one that made them cry (or one that caused them to struggle holding in their tears). If you don't know, then look over the movies in these chapters and find one that you can identify with.

You may notice that there are more classic movies than recent movies. Someone said it well when they said that the absolute best movies are the classic movies. Chances are, many of you have never heard of some of them, but they are still available for streaming. Don't make the mistake of bypassing a great movie just because you've never heard of it or just because it may be in black and white.

I also want to give a disclaimer that most of these movies were selected by clients and friends when asked what made them cry.

If you ever wonder why a particular movie was selected as a cry movie, you'll have to trust me that someone said it was their cry movie. Also, feel free to send me your personal selection if it's not on the list and I'll consider writing updates to this book. My email is: cryingbook22@gmail.com.

12

Abandonment Movies

When watching movies that have characters dealing with feelings of abandonment, we are able to get in touch with our own feelings of abandonment.

Bolt (2008) PG

> I have never seen this animated movie, but I will never forget the middle school girl who told me that this was her cry movie. Bolt is a dog who is also an actor. The problem is that he thinks he really is the superhero dog that he portrays. He also thinks it's his job to protect Penny, the girl he is always saving in their TV series. One of the episodes has Penny being kidnapped. Bolt, thinking it is really happening and that he needs to save her, sets out to find her. He has an accident and falls in a box of foam peanuts (unconscious) and ends up getting shipped to New York City. He sets out to find his way back home to Penny. The scene that made my client cry was when Bolt finally made it back to the set one day and

realized that he had been replaced with another dog acting as the new superhero.

Charlie St. Cloud (2010) PG-13

Just watching the trailer of this movie will bring you to tears. The main character, Charlie (Zac Efron), is grieving the death of his younger (and only) brother, Sam (Charlie Tahan). Townspeople think that Charlie has gone nuts because he continues to carry on a relationship with Sam, who appears to him quite regularly. One of Charlie's former classmates, Tess (Amanda Crew) comes back into his life. Now he has a decision to make; follow his heart into his future or remain stuck in the world of his brother.

Hope Floats (1998) PG-13

Birdee Pruitt (Sandra Bullock) has been humiliated on live television by her best friend, Connie, who's been sleeping with Birdee's husband. Birdee tries starting over with her daughter, Bernice (Mae Whitman) by returning to her small Texas hometown, but she's faced with petty old acquaintances who are thrilled to see her unhappy—except for her longtime friend Justin (Harry Connick, Jr.). Love takes hold as Justin helps Birdee get back on her feet again. For anyone with childhood abandonment issues, this is usually the movie they name as their main cry movie.

I Can Only Imagine (2018) PG

This is a true story about the lead singer of Christian band MercyMe, Bart Millard (J. Michael Finley). Bart suffered from a physically and emotionally abusive father, Arthur (Dennis Quaid). This movie tells the story of how he coped with the abuse and how he mended his relationship with his dad, after his dad finds faith in God. Bart later writes the hit song, "I Can Only Imagine."

Second Hand Lions (2003) PG

This is a must-see movie. Young Walter (Haley Joel Osment) is left by his mom with his two older feisty uncles (Michael Caine and Robert Duvall)—who are believed to be very wealthy—in a run-down old house. These uncles really don't want Walter around since he is afraid of his own shadow. However, the three eventually bond and they tell Walter stories of their past. Walter helps them lighten up and have more fun. Even though this is a light-hearted and fun movie to watch, the way Walter's mother (Kyra Sedgwick) flippantly abandons him and lies to him is what touches the heart of those who have also been abandoned.

The Brave Little Toaster (1987) NR

This was one of my daughter's favorite movies when she was little. This is an animated film about five household appliances who have been left in an abandoned cabin. When they get overwhelmingly lonely, they decide to go find their long-lost owner and survive as best as they can on their way. They finally arrive in a big city and realize how outdated they are because of new, more modern appliances.

Up (2009) PG

This is a cute, animated movie that I recommend everyone watch. The tearful part happens at the start of the movie when elderly Carl loses the love of his life. Left all alone without anyone or anything to cheer him up, he decides to attach thousands of balloons to his house, and he takes off and floats his house to South America. This is to fulfill a dream he and his wife had of living there one day. During this flight, he discovers a young boy scout named Russell has stowed away on the porch of his house. Along comes Dug, the dog they discover, and the fun begins.

Uptown Girls (2003) PG-13

This is a cute movie that seems like a comedy but deals with a serious issue. A privileged and spoiled adult, Molly (Brittany Murphy)—whose father is a famous rock star—never really grew up. When she discovers that her manager stole all her money and left her destitute, she finds a job as a nanny to a young girl, Ray (Dakota Fanning)—who is like an adult in a child's body. At first these two don't get along, but as they get to know each other, they begin to bond. Molly helps Ray lighten up and be more childlike, and Ray helps Molly grow up and be more responsible. There are touching moments during the movie. Both girls deal with emotional abandonment from the adults in their lives.

13

Childhood/Family Issues Movies

Many hurtful things happen in a child's life that never get resolved and are carried around into adulthood. Watching movies that depict these issues helps us find release of our own childhood issues and allows us to finally grieve these hurts. Also, movies dealing with issues that happen among families will help us get in touch with unresolved issues we have from our past.

A Monster Calls (2016) PG-13

> This movie was recommended to me by a male client who had gone through a tough time in his childhood during his parent's contentious divorce. This was his cry movie. I was blown away when I watched it. In the movie, an adolescent boy named Conor (Lewis MacDougall) is bullied and an outcast at his school, while he is dealing with a very ill mother (Felicity Jones) and an overbearing grandmother (Sigourney Weaver). His father (Toby Kebbell) lives in another country far away. He gets a visit by a Monster (Liam Neeson) over and over, who becomes Conor's guide on his journey of courage, faith, and truth.

Bed of Roses (1996) PG

A very painful childhood caused Lisa (Mary Stuart Masterson) to be shut down emotionally. She has become a workaholic and the last thing she is looking for is a relationship. However, when she is sent an anonymous bouquet of flowers, she goes to the florist to find out who sent them. After getting to know her better, the florist, Louis (Christian Slater), admits that he was the one who sent them, and he quickly sweeps Lisa off her feet. He also experienced a painful past. Will they be able to help each other overcome their pasts?

Bridge to Terabithia (2007) PG

Two adolescents, Jesse (Josh Hutcherson) and Leslie (AnnaSophia Robb) help each other through their difficult lives by creating an imaginary world called Terabithia, where all sorts of magical creatures reside. Their ordinary lives are wrought with difficulties, but this doesn't stop them from creating a mystical world where they become king and queen. It is this imaginary strength that one of them must draw on when faced with a tragic event.

Inside Out (2015) PG

This is my favorite movie to discuss as a counselor. Both children and adults all understand the concept that we have emotions running through our brain, or our "Control Centers," at all times. Riley, an eleven-year-old girl who is uprooted from her home and moved to a new town clear across the country from her friends, tries to navigate her new lonely life. She experiences many emotions that are difficult to deal with. This is a comedy that will have you laughing many times—yet, has some deeply moving parts that will bring you to tears.

Irreconcilable Differences (1984) PG

This is a sad movie about a couple (Ryan O'Neal and Shelley Long) who have a little girl, Casey (Drew Barrymore) that they don't pay much attention to. They are both more concerned with their careers. In the meantime, Casey grows very close to the housekeeper, Maria (Hortensia Colorado), because that's who her parents always leave her with. She decides to sue her parents for divorce and is granted custody to Maria and moves in with Maria's family. For those who identify with Casey, this is their cry movie because she is invisible to her parents but does something to get their attention.

Kramer vs. Kramer (1979) PG

This movie is hard to watch. A mom, Joanna (Meryl Streep) walks away from her husband, Ted (Dustin Hoffman) and child, Billy (Justin Henry). Ted and Billy somehow manage to move on. Then Joanna returns over a year later and takes Ted to court to get her child back. The court grants custody to Joanna, and Ted is devastated. Watch until the end to see how it turns out.

Life As a House (2001) R

George (Kevin Kline) is in trouble. His son, Sam (Hayden Christensen) hates him and is suicidal, he's just lost his job, then he finds out that he has cancer with only a few months to live. He sets out to tear down his house and forces his son to help him. As they start to rebuild this house, family relationships start to get rebuilt. This will tug at your heartstrings as you see Sam's emotional struggle at the end.

Mystic River (2003) R

While I have not personally seen this movie, it has been recommended to me as someone's cry movie. The main characters are played by Sean Penn, Tim Robbins, and Kevin Bacon. The movie involves some sensitive themes, including child sexual abuse with murder and violence. It has strong performances and was nominated for several academy awards. Read the reviews and watch the trailer, because if this is something you had to deal with in childhood, it will strike some emotional nerves.

Ordinary People (1980) R

This movie deals with the topic of PTSD (Post Traumatic Stress Disorder) and Survivor's Guilt. Conrad (Timothy Hutton) is the son who returns home after four months in a psychiatric hospital following his own suicide attempt after the accidental death of his older brother, Buck. Conrad was involved in the sailing accident that caused Buck's death and he struggles to live with this guilt. His mother, Beth (Mary Tyler Moore) is in major denial of Buck's loss, and she tries to get her family back together. This is a difficult movie to watch, but for those who have had family trauma, it is a must see.

Stand By Me (1986) R

It's been years since I've seen this coming-of-age film about four boys (played by River Phoenix, Wil Wheaton, Jerry O'Connell and Corey Feldman) who set out to find a dead body that they heard was seen near their hometown. While on this trek, they get to know each other better and learn about their different home lives. They finally discover the body and anonymously report it to the police, but more important than that was the bond they created over this life-defining event.

Still Alice (2014) PG-13

Alice (Julianne Moore) is a fifty-year-old English professor with a husband and three grown children when she starts having problems with her memory. During a class lecture, she suddenly forgets what she was saying, and another time she gets lost while jogging on campus. She goes to her doctor, who diagnoses her with early onset Alzheimer's. Alice comes up with ways to help her keep her memory, even making a video to herself with suicide directions in case she ever gets so bad she loses all her memory. This movie does a fantastic job of showing the ugly truth of Alzheimer's and how a person's memory deteriorates. If you've ever had to watch a loved one go through something like this, this movie will help you release lots of emotions as you watch it. Guaranteed to bring out those tears. Great movie.

The Father (2020) PG-13

Taking care of aging parents is very difficult. Dealing with dementia or Alzheimer's is overwhelming as we watch them deteriorate into someone we don't recognize while they gradually don't recognize us. The father is Anthony Hopkins, who does an excellent job as a pompous know-it-all who believes he has no problems with his memory but is losing it at the same time.

The Kid (2000) PG

I dragged my parents to the theater to watch this movie after I saw it, because I wanted them to see my job on film. I help clients view their childhood with adult eyes and rethink any misconceptions they have about themselves. This comedy movie is about a man, Russ (Bruce Willis) who is a complete jerk, but highly successful, nonetheless. He gets a visit from his eight-year-old self, Rusty (Spencer Breslin), who ends up walking him through a past trauma he experienced at age eight. Watching his childhood trauma with adult eyes causes him to realize it wasn't his fault and he is able to become a nice guy again. It is highly entertaining and funny yet carries a much deeper meaning. I recommend you watch this movie because you won't be disappointed. Lily Tomlin and Jean Smart bring some hilarity and fun.

Then She Found Me (2007) R

This movie has one of my favorite actresses so I (of course) loved it. It's interesting to watch all the emotions April (Helen Hunt) goes through in this movie as her life falls apart then comes together then falls apart again. April meets her birth mother, Bernice (Bette Midler), who is nothing like April. If you have struggled with pregnancy issues, death of someone you love, or adoption/birth mother issues, this movie will most definitely strike a few of your emotional nerves.

What Maisie Knew (2012) R

This is a must-see for anyone with children who go through a divorce. This movie does an excellent job of showing the child, Maisie's (Onata Aprile) point of view. Even though Maisie's parents tell her they love her, Maisie can tell that their careers are more important to them than she is. Excellent acting and portrayal of the intense emotions children go through when parents fight.

When A Man Loves a Woman (1994) R

This is a wonderful movie dealing with alcoholism but can be difficult to watch. Alice (Meg Ryan) is a school counselor with two children: nine-year-old Jess (Tina Majorino) from a previous marriage, and four-year-old Casey (Mae Whitman) from her current marriage to Michael (Andy Garcia). Michael is an airline pilot and is often away from home. Alice has a serious drinking problem and finally agrees to get help after a bad episode. She works hard to overcome this with help, and is able to return home. However, the marriage suffers. Great actors make this movie interesting to watch. If you've ever had to deal with alcoholism in your family or life, this is the movie you need to see.

White Oleander (2020) PG-13

This is the movie for those who have had a dysfunctional mother/daughter relationship. It's excellently acted and hits so many emotional wounds for those who have recommended it to me. I've heard from clients that it had them crying at several parts in the movie. Michelle Pfeiffer plays the mom and Alison Lohman plays her daughter.

14

Feel Good Movies

If life is especially difficult for you, watching a feel-good movie can bring you to tears. Unfulfilled dreams you may have, or just wishing your life was going better can cause tears. There are many wonderful movies for this category, but I only listed a few favorites here.

Cool Runnings (1993) PG

> This movie is quite funny with the excellent comedic actors in it. John Candy plays a washed-up and disgraced bobsled champion who agrees to take on four men from Jamaica who have never even seen snow, much less know how to steer a bobsled. I thought it was a true story but found out not much of it was true. Nevertheless, it was fun to watch. Enjoy the lightheartedness of this movie and maybe you will shed a few happy tears along the way.

Courageous (2011) PG-13

This is a Christian-based movie about four policemen who, because of personal family issues, decide to become better fathers by all signing a resolution to put family first and follow God. The outcome is uplifting. This is a very encouraging movie that all fathers should watch. It stars Alex Kendrick, Ken Bevel, Kevin Downes and Rusty Martin.

Facing The Giants (2006) PG

Grant (Alex Kendrick) and Brook (Shannen Fields) are struggling financially and struggling to conceive a child. Added to that is the fact that Grant—a high school football coach—is about to lose his job. He turns his life over to God and changes start happening. Watch this movie until the end. If you have a heart, you'll most likely be crying happy tears.

Fireproof (2008) PG

Caleb (Kirk Cameron) is a hero to everyone in town except his wife, Catherine (Erin Bethea). They have drifted apart as a couple and fight more than they talk. Caleb is a firefighter and he and his fellow firefighters are a close-knit group. As Caleb discusses the problems he's facing at home, they all give him good advice on how to save his marriage. Caleb mentions to his dad that he wants a divorce—but his dad asks him to hold off from that for 40 days. His dad then sends him "The Love Dare" book and asks Caleb to take things one day at a time. If you are married, this movie will encourage you to be a better partner to your spouse.

Gifted Hands (2009) NR

Based on the life of Dr. Ben Carson (Cuba Gooding, Jr.), this is a wonderful movie to watch with your family; but if you need to cry, watch it alone. Poor and unmotivated, young Ben Carson had a mother who inspired both her boys to do better and use the gifts they possessed. She had them turn in book reports to her each week, even though she didn't know how to read. Ben succeeded as a student and soared to the top of his classes. He was awarded a scholarship to Yale University where he met his wife, Candy (Aunjanue Ellis). He studied neuroscience and was accepted as a resident at Johns Hopkins Hospital. His impressive career as a neurosurgeon garnered him fame among doctors. A particularly difficult surgery where he had to separate two conjoined twins is highlighted. This is a refreshing and inspiring movie that will bring happy tears to viewers.

Hoosiers (1986) PG

Coach Norman Dale (Gene Hackman) is hired to help a struggling high school basketball team in a small Indiana town. He is criticized by the townspeople (and dads of his players) for his temper and for being washed up. He has a friend in one of the teachers there, Myra (Barbara Hershey), who he develops a relationship with. This is a great movie to watch, especially if you love to pull for the underdogs.

It's a Wonderful Life (1946) PG

This is my absolute favorite Christmas movie. I wasn't sure what category to put it in, because it's sort of bittersweet. George Bailey (Jimmy Stewart) dreams of traveling the world and building things, but due to his father's untimely death, he must take over the family savings and loan or it will be shut down. He agrees to forego college and work there while his younger brother goes off to college. The plan is to have his brother come home to take over so he can go to college later. However, his brother ends up getting married and taking a job with his father-in-law. George feels stuck and unfulfilled. But things change when Mary Hatch (Donna Reed) comes back to town, and they fall in love and marry. But calamity strikes when Uncle Billy (Thomas Mitchell) loses a huge deposit for the savings & loan and greedy miser Henry Potter (Lionel Barrymore) finds it and keeps it. This is a great depiction of what one man's life can mean to the people he meets during his life. George gets a chance to see what his town would be like had he never been born. Amazing performance by Clarence Odbody (Henry Travers). This movie needs to be on your bucket list of great movies to watch.

Miracle On Ice (1981) NR

This is an inspiring movie that details the 1980 U.S. Men's Olympic Hockey Team, coached by Herb Brooks (Karl Malden). It's exciting to watch, even knowing that they end up winning the gold medal against the favored Soviet team. It's what happens to get them to be winners that makes this movie special.

Overcomer (2019) PG

This movie is very inspirational. It a Christian based film full of hope and encouragement. The message is loud and clear that God has a plan for everyone and when you trust Him, you will not be disappointed. In the movie, a high school basketball coach, John (Alex Kendrick), is discouraged when the town's largest manufacturing firm shuts down and people start to move away. John no longer has enough players for his basketball team. But John agrees to be the new track coach. His only athlete is Hannah, (Aryn Wright Thompson) a cross-country runner, who pushes herself to the limit as she prepares for the race of her life. This movie provides laughter along with tears.

Pay It Forward (2007) PG-13

Eugene (Kevin Spacey) is a social studies teacher who assigns his students the task of finding a way to change the world for the better and put this plan into action. One of his students, Trevor (Haley Joel Osment), comes up with a plan to "pay forward" favors, which assists his struggling single mother Arlene (Helen Hunt). Eventually his plan creates a wave of human kindness that explodes into a profound national phenomenon. This movie not only touches you emotionally, but it also challenges you to make something special of your world.

The Blind Side (2009) PG

Definitely one of my favorite movies. It is based on the true story of Michael Oher (Quinton Aaron), who becomes a star offensive player in the NFL (National Football League). Homeless and practically illiterate, he is taken in by Sean (Tim McGraw) and Leigh Anne Tuohy (Sandra Bullock). They adopt him, provide tutors for him, and sign him up to play football, where he eventually excels. This movie will produce tears, some sad and some happy.

The War Room (2015) PG

This is my favorite movie by the Kendrick brothers. I had no idea what it was about until I watched it. A realtor, Elizabeth (Priscilla Shirer) realizes that her husband Tony (T.C. Stallings) is drifting away. They have an enviable lifestyle but looks can be deceiving. When Elizbeth meets Clara (Karen Abercrombie), she learns the secret to a happy marriage: prayer. This movie will have you in tears as you watch the struggles this family goes through, and the way God changes everything for the better.

We Are Marshall (2006) PG

Excellent and uplifting, the movie opens with a tragedy almost too horrible to believe. This movie tells the true story of what happened back in 1970. Marshall University, in Huntington, WV, lost its entire football team and staff (seventy-five people total) in a horrible plane crash. Jack Lengyel (Matthew McConaughey) hires on as the new head coach and slowly rebuilds the team and the community as they recover from this disaster.

15

Grief and Loss Movies

This is the largest category since it deals with one of the main emotions in eliciting tears—sadness. Watching sad movies is one of the best ways for us to get in touch with unresolved loss in our own lives.

A Walk to Remember (2002) PG

> This movie is a winner. Jamie (Mandy Moore) is an outcast at school because she could care less about fashion or popularity. She is more interested in doing what is right—something the other kids often bully her about. When Landon (Shane West), the popular "bad boy" gets in serious trouble and is given a choice of being expelled or doing community service (including being in the school play), he opts for community service. Landon doesn't know how to act, so he reluctantly asks for help from Jamie. He begins going to her house to practice. Watch to see what develops and the impact Jamie's life has on Landon. It's a tearjerker, for sure.

Always (1989) PG

This movie was recommended by an adult male who said this was his cry movie. It's about a pilot named Pete (Richard Dreyfuss) who was taking dangerous missions in his plane—putting out forest fires. His girlfriend Dorinda (Holly Hunter), also a pilot, wants him to stop because she is afraid he will be killed. He takes one last flight and, while saving fellow pilot and best friend Al (John Goodman), who's plane catches fire, Pete loses control and ends up getting killed. Pete, after death, becomes a spirit guide to help others. Unbeknownst to Belinda, Pete helps her through a dangerous mission of her own, then on the way home, is able to tell her everything he never got to say to her. In the end, he sets her free to follow her heart. Directed by Stephen Spielberg, this is definitely one you will remember.

Bang The Drum Slowly (1973) PG

This is a very moving story about a Major League Baseball (MLB) pitcher, Henry (Michael Moriarty) and MLB catcher, Bruce (Robert De Niro), who develop a strong friendship. Bruce learns that he has Hodgkin's Disease and is dying, but Henry fights to keep him on the team as his catcher without revealing his illness to anyone. Eventually, they find out and all pull together as a team in support of Bruce. The tenderness, honesty, and even humor in this movie is sure to bring on the tears.

Beaches (1988) PG-13

You cannot watch this movie without a box of tissues on hand. If you've ever loved a friend, you need to see this movie. Excellent acting with lots of humor, it packs a punch when tragedy strikes. Barbara Hershey and Bette Midler make a great team as Hillary and Cece. This movie is usually on most women's cry movie list.

Beyond Borders (2003) R

This is an intense movie that can be difficult to watch. It has been listed as someone's cry movie due to the romance and heartbreak between Sarah (Angelina Jolie) and Nick (Clive Owen). Sarah is an American socialite who leaves everything behind after she meets Nick, who is a doctor in Africa. She travels there to help with the refugee effort and quickly falls in love but stays with Nick no matter the danger and risk to her own life.

Big Fish (2003) PG-13

This is a rather strange, but interesting movie to watch. To better get to know his father Edward (Albert Finney), journalist William (Billy Crudup) begins to investigate all the tall tales his father told him as he grew up. After Edward's death, he begins to understand his father more and why he always had to tell stories.

Bryan's Song (1971) NR

This is a true story that I watched in middle school. I still remember crying my eyes out even then. Gale Sayers (Billy Dee Williams) joins the Chicago Bears and is befriended by Brian Piccolo (James Caan), an over-achieving running back. Although they compete for the same spot on the team, and even though Sayers is black and Piccolo white, they become roommates on the road and very close friends, especially when Sayers is injured, and Piccolo helps in his recovery. Later, they and their wives must deal with the harsh reality of Piccolo's cancer.

City of Angels (1998) PG-13

Seth (Nicholas Cage) is an angel that has been sent to help people who are dying, make the transition to their next life. Humans cannot see him—only those who are dying. During one of the transitions, he notices one doctor in particular named Maggie (Meg Ryan) who is upset over losing her patient. Even though she is not near death, he becomes visible to her. They develop a connection that turns into attraction. Seth learns that angels can become human again and he is told how to do this. He becomes a human and goes to find Maggie, who is on vacation. He finds his way there and lets her know he has become human. They make love that night, but the next morning, happy Maggie is feeling great and rides her bike to the store. On the way, she has an accident that changes everything.

Crouching Tiger Hidden Dragon (2000) PG-13

This was listed as a cry movie by an adult male. Though this movie does have lots of martial arts and special effects in it, the romance, story line, scenery and great acting are what stands out in this movie. It is a beautiful and exquisite movie to watch. Starring Michelle Yeoh, Zhang Ziyi and Chow Yun-fat.

Dad (1989) PG

I saw this movie years ago and still remember how touching it was. John (Ted Danson) takes care of his aging dad (Jack Lemmon) after his mother dies. His dad moves in with him and their relationship starts off a bit awkwardly for John. Eventually, as John cares for his dad, he begins to realize that he needs to work on his relationship with his own son (Ethan Hawke). This movie will touch your heart and your tears will flow.

Dead Poets Society (1989) PG

John (Robin Williams) is an unorthodox teacher at an all-boys prep school. Forgetting the school's traditions and standards, he connects with his students in a way that helps them understand life a little better, set goals for themselves, and break out of their shells. There are life lessons to be learned not just by the characters in the movie, but for those watching as well.

Dear John (2010) PG-13

A strong romance begins when soldier John Tyree (Channing Tatum) meets an idealistic college student, Savannah Curtis (Amanda Seyfried). Because of John's dangerous deployments, they can only communicate by letters over the next seven years (meeting in person only a few times). Their correspondence triggers consequences that they hadn't expected. Heartwarming, but sad, it's guaranteed to pull your heart strings.

Doctor Zhivago (1965) PG-13

This movie is touted as one of the greatest movies of all time. It is longer than most movies, running over three hours, but it is packed with action and romance. Filmed in Russia, it has beautiful scenes and story lines even with a revolution going on. The acting is fantastic, the story is compelling, and if your heart isn't torn out at the end, you may find it wasn't there in the first place. Starring Julie Christie and Omar Sharif.

Extremely Loud and Incredibly Close (2011) PG-13

This is a very emotional movie about a boy, Oskar (Thomas Horn), who loses his father (Tom Hanks) in the 9/11 attack on the World Trade Center. Because of their close relationship, he believes that his dad has left him a message somewhere in the city and sets out to discover what it is. His journey helps him move past his loss to a new understanding of his world. When you lose a loved one unexpectedly, you search for closure that you may never find. This movie shows the length that Oskar went to find closure with his dad. Your emotions will be carried along as he seeks to find his answers. Also stars Sandra Bullock as Oskar's mother.

Field of Dreams (1989) PG

This is a movie that men have told me they get emotional watching. It is about a farmer from Iowa, Ray (Kevin Costner), who hears a voice one night saying to him, "If you build it, he will come." He's not sure what it is but feels compelled to act on it. Not concerned that all the townspeople think he's crazy, he begins to build a fully lit baseball diamond in his cornfield. With his wife Annie's (Amy Madigan) support, he continues building the field even with looming financial problems. Once the field is built, the ghosts of former great ball players start coming to play on it. The lesson for Ray is much more than watching former greats play. Also a great performance by James Earl Jones.

Finding Neverland (2004) PG

I happened to watch this delightful movie years ago, not knowing that it was basically the true story of James M. Barrie, author of *Peter Pan*. James (Johnny Depp) happens to meet a widow (Kate Winslet) with four boys in a park one day and finds in the boys the inspiration to create Neverland. He helps the boys overcome their grief and learn to use their imagination. In an emotional scene, James tells young Peter (Freddie Highmore) that "You can visit Neverland any time you like." With tears in his eyes, Little Peter asks how? James replies: "By believing, Peter." An inspirational movie to anyone who has loved and lost.

Forrest Gump (1994) PG-13

I saw this movie just after it had come out in theaters with my late husband. I remember walking out of it and looking at him and saying I wasn't sure I understood this movie, but I was definitely entertained by it. It's about the life of a boy, Forrest (Tom Hanks) who starts out not only a bit slow mentally, but also crippled and having to wear leg braces. One day when he is running along, his leg braces fall off and he ends up being a champion runner. He has life experiences that defy explanation—being a college football star, a hero in Vietnam, or working on a shrimp boat with his friend, Captain Dan (Gary Sinise). Of most importance to Forrest is his longtime best childhood friend, Jenny (Robin Wright)—who grows up to be a hippie and finds herself in trouble. Forrest sets out to save her. There are a few tearful moments that grab your heart. Also starring Sally Field as Forrest's mother.

Ghost (1990) PG-13

This is a bittersweet love story that stays with you long after the movie is over. Sam (Patrick Swayze) has it all: a great job, a great girlfriend, Molly (Demi Moore), and a newly renovated apartment. Sam is murdered by his "friend" and business partner Carl (Tony Goldwyn) and ends up as a ghost who cannot communicate with anyone. He finally finds a psychic, Oda Mae (Whoopi Goldberg), who can hear him but not see him. With her help, he is able to protect Molly and discover the ones responsible for his death. Anyone who has ever lost someone they loved will have their emotional catharsis by watching this movie.

Hero (1992) PG-13

This is not just another great Dustin Hoffman movie. It is also a true picture of human nature. Bernie (Dustin Hoffman) is a lowlife swindler, divorced with a ten-year-old son he rarely sees. Then one night he witnesses a plane crash from the road and decides to help save injured passengers. Covered in mud, he leaves unnoticed. When reporter Gale (Geena Davis)—who was one of the passengers that was saved—announces a one-million-dollar reward for finding the hero, an imposter—John (Andy Garcia)—comes forward. Bernie sets out to expose this imposter. Watch this movie to see if the truth will prevail in the end.

How Green Was My Valley (1941) G

This movie is a heart-warming story about the Morgan family, coal miners living in a Welsh mining town. Roddy McDowall is Huw, the youngest Morgan son. A miner's strike causes division in the Morgan family because the sons want improvements in the mines, but their father doesn't want to cause a stir. This is a model family, who go through struggles like we all do. Watching this movie, we become drawn into their lives and easily feel their emotions.

Love Comes Softly (2003) NR

This was my catharsis movie the year after my husband died. I had no idea what this movie was about, but I also had no idea how much sadness I was holding on to. This is a beautiful story, based on a Janette Oke novel. Katherine Heigl plays Marty, who just moved out west with her husband. Before they reach their destination, he is killed in an accident. Alone and pregnant, she needs a place to stay for the winter. She reluctantly accepts a proposal of marriage from widower Clark (Dale Midkiff), who needs someone to look after his young daughter, Missie (Skye McCole). Watch this

SALLY SCOTT CREED, LPC-S, RPT-S

movie to see how the story unfolds. This is the first movie in a series.

Love Is a Many Splendored Thing (1955) NR

This is an oldie but a goodie. During the Chinese civil war, Mark (William Holden) is an American reporter in Hong Kong who is separated from his wife. He meets Dr. Han (Jennifer Jones), and they fall in love despite disapproval from his friends and her family. This is a heart-breaking movie about love and war.

Love Story (1970) PG

Released in 1970, this is one of the most romantic movies of all time. This movie originated the phrase "Love means never having to say you're sorry." Oliver (Ryan O'Neal), a wealthy Harvard law student, meets a middle-class student from Radcliffe named Jenny (Ali MacGraw). Conflict arises with Ryan's father (Ray Milland), who is opposed to this relationship. Despite him, they marry anyway. Oliver is hired at a law firm in New York, but their happiness is short-lived when they discover that Jenny has a terminal illness. A definite tearjerker.

Magnolia (1999) R

This is another movie that is just over three hours long. This was listed as someone's cry movie because of Jason Robards' scenes where he talks about his regrets. I wasn't sure I wanted to watch this movie, but the reviews on it were outstanding. If you'd like to watch this movie, please make sure you have the time in your day to watch the entire movie in one sitting in order to get the full effect. Excellent performances by Tom Cruise, Julianne Moore, Phillip Seymour, John C. Reilly, and William H. Macy.

Meet Joe Black (1998) PG-13

This movie will grab you right from the start. It is a love story with a quirky twist: Joe (Brad Pitt) is Death dressed as a handsome young man. He suddenly appears in media tycoon Bill Parrish's (Anthony Hopkins) life. He goes everywhere with Bill—board meetings, family dinners, and even lives in his house. He falls in love with Bill's daughter Susan (Claire Forlani) who is a successful doctor. Joe is sent to earth to guide Bill to the next world, but no one knows this except Bill. The end is extremely emotional. This is an unforgettable movie with superb acting.

Message In a Bottle (1999) PG-13

A wonderful love story about a woman journalist Theresa Osborne (Robin Wright Penn) who finds a bottle while jogging on the beach. The bottle has an anonymous love letter in it that breaks her heart. She publishes it in her paper, then successfully tracks down the author of the letter, reclusive widower Garret Blake (Kevin Costner). She meets him, then falls in love with him, but will it last? Beautiful scenery, excellent acting, and totally heartbreaking.

Moulin Rouge (2001) PG-13

I saw this movie shortly after it came out. It is a highly entertaining yet tragic love story. It's a musical about a poor writer (Ewan McGregor) who falls in love with a singer (Nicole Kidman), who has a secret she is hiding. Before they can finally get together, his heart is broken and so is yours.

My All American (2015) PG

This is a wonderful true story that I watched a few years ago. Freddie (Finn Wittrock) accepts a football scholarship to University of Texas at Austin in the late 1960s and is excited to be playing for coach Darrell Royal (Aaron Eckhart). There is quite a bit of football action for all the football lovers out there. Freddie helps the UT Longhorns to a successful season but suffers a serious injury. When he finally goes in for treatment, he finds out that he has leg cancer that ends his career. He is an inspiration to his teammates. I cried my eyes out watching his bravery and all the love and support he got from those who knew him.

My Girl (1991) PG

This is a sweet but tragic story between two eleven-year-old best friends, Vada (Anna Chlumsky) and Thomas (Macaulay Culkin). Vada lives with her father at a funeral home he owns. Her mother died a couple of days after she was born. She has developed anxiety and has become a hypochondriac, thinking she will die. Thomas is a boy she hangs out with who is allergic to everything. He accompanies her to her doctor visits so the doctor can tell Vada that she is not sick. A tragic accident happens that separates the best friends, and it is heart wrenching to watch a child grieve a loss like this.

My Life (1993) PG-13

With Michael Keaton (Bob) and Nicole Kidman (Gail) in a movie, you're guaranteed to be entertained. This movie does not disappoint. Bob and Gail are expecting their first child, but Bob finds out he has cancer and won't live to meet his son. He videotapes himself talking to his son while he does various things because he wants his son to know who he is. But Bob is determined to live long enough to see his son. What he discovers about himself will touch your emotional heartstrings.

Nights In Rodanthe (2008) PG-13

This is one of my favorites. Adrienne (Diane Lane) agrees to take care of a friend's inn for the weekend in the small coastal town of Rodanthe, NC. She wants to be alone to sort out her chaotic life. There is only one guest, Dr. Paul Flanner (Richard Gere), who is dealing with his own demons. Things heat up as a massive storm approaches and Adrienne and Paul must help each other through it. They both find comfort and romance that neither of them expected.

Of Mice and Men (1992) PG-13

This is an excellent adaptation of the novel by John Steinbeck. George (Gary Sinise) is an itinerant worker who travels with his mentally challenged friend, Lennie (John Malkovich) as they look for work during the Great Depression. The way George protects Lennie from bullies is heartwarming. Their dream is to own their own ranch, and they are given an opportunity to own part of a ranch, but Lennie's fascination with the owner's daughter-in-law (Sherilyn Fenn) almost destroys their dreams.

P.S. I Love You (2007) PG-13

When Holly's (Hilary Swank) husband Gerry (Gerard Butler) dies from an illness, she is devastated. Gerry was the great love of her life. Gerry knew how difficult this would be for Holly, so he planned ahead and wrote several letters to be sent to her on various occasions, beginning with her thirtieth birthday. His hope was to ease her grief and encourage her to move on with her life. The romantic scenes will bring you to tears, the beautiful scenery will overwhelm you, and the ending will surprise you.

Return To Me (2000) PG

One of my favorites! This movie has it all: laughter, tears, romance, and intense friendships. It's fun to watch, but don't be fooled by all the hilarity. It will have you crying within the first ten minutes of the movie. Bob Rueland (David Duchovny) is heartbroken and shut down emotionally after the death of his beloved wife. His friend, Charlie (David Alan Grier), wants to set Bob up on blind dates, but Bob refuses to go. He finally relents one time and instead of noticing his date, he notices the waitress, Grace (Minnie Driver). Grace is a recovering heart transplant patient who is hesitant to go out with anyone because of her scar. When Bob discovers the secret Grace carries, their romance grows even stronger.

Shenandoah (1965) NR

This is my husband's cry movie because the subject matter hits him very close to home. During the American Civil War, a wealthy widower (Jimmy Stewart) is opposed to war on moral grounds. Yet he is forced to get involved because his youngest son is captured by the Union army, his son-in-law is chosen to serve in the Confederate forces, and another son and pregnant daughter-in-law are killed by looters. Any movie with Jimmy Stewart in it is a winner, but the ending of this movie will tear your heart out, especially if you've lost a loved one to war, as my husband did. Also stars Doug McClure, Glenn Corbett, and Patrick Wayne.

Steel Magnolias (1989) PG

As you may have seen on earlier pages, this is my top number one cry movie. I'll share why: I've always loved Sally Field because she's a great actress and she has my name (or I have hers). Plus, in this movie, she's a therapist - which is what I am. She has a daughter with diabetes, and I have a daughter with OI (Osteogenesis Imperfecta—or Brittle Bones). She was an overprotective mother and so was I, even though my daughter is doing well now. When I needed to cry, I would watch this movie and just sob and sob (and laugh a lot). M'Lynn (Sally Field) is planning a wedding for her daughter, Shelby (Julia Roberts). M'Lynn's friends all share in the fun and hilarity of each other's lives: Ouiser Boudreaux (Shirley MacLaine), Truvy Jones (Dolly Parton), Clairee Belcher (Olympia Dukakis), and Annelle Dupuis (Daryl Hannah). But when tragedy strikes Shelby, the women all get together to support M'Lynn through it. If you've never seen this movie, do yourself a favor and move it to the top of your must-see list.

Stepmom (1998) PG-13

Don't skip this movie because you know it's a tearjerker. There are plenty of funny and entertaining scenes throughout to keep you smiling. Jackie (Susan Sarandon) is the mother of Luke's (Ed Harris) two kids. When Luke moves his new fashion photographer girlfriend, Kelly (Julia Roberts), in with him, trouble ensues. The children have a strong bond with their mom, and they reject any attempts to bond with Kelly. But when there is a family crisis, things begin to change.

Terms of Endearment (1983) PG

Emma (Debra Winger) married Flap Horton (Jeff Daniels) against her widowed mom's wishes. Her mom, Aurora (Shirley MacLaine), lets Emma and her three children move in with her when Emma and Flap split up. Not long after, Emma learns that she has terminal cancer. As she deteriorates, Aurora is by her side in the hospital as Emma tries to make peace with Flap and her children before she dies. This is extremely emotional and an excellent cry movie for anyone dealing with the untimely death of a child (or a mom).

The Champ (1979) PG

I've seen this movie once a very long time ago. It tore my heart out then and it will most likely tear yours out as well. When TJ's (Ricky Schroeder) mom Annie (Faye Dunaway) leaves the family, his dad Billy (Jon Voight) does his best to care for him. Billy used to be a great boxer, but now he's training horses, drinking too much, and enjoying being with TJ. But when Annie comes back and wants TJ back, Billy goes back in the boxing ring to try and revive his successful boxing career.

The Evening Star (1996) PG-13

This movie is a sequel to another movie on my list: *Terms of Endearment* —so I would suggest that you watch that first, so you know the storyline. But this movie can stand alone if you want to watch it anyway. Aurora (Shirley MacLaine) struggles to raise her three grandchildren all by herself after their mother dies, but they don't turn out quite the way she expected. Filled with humor, frustration, angst, and ultimately love, this movie will win your heart. Jack Nicholson and Juliette Lewis also star.

The Notebook (2004) PG-13

I would rate this movie as the top cry movie recommendation of the century. It is deeply moving and romantic. I was affected by the intensity of the love that Noah (Ryan Gosling) and Allie (Rachel McAdams) had for each other. In the 1940s, Noah was a mill worker who fell in love with rich girl Allie. Her parents didn't want her with Noah, so the couple broke it off before Noah went off to fight in WWII. Years later, Noah returns to town just before Allie is getting ready to be married to someone else. Once they meet, they realize that they belong together. Beautiful movie with a beautiful ending.

Untamed Heart (1993) PG-13

Casting Marisa Tomei (Caroline) and Christian Slater (Adam) in this movie was brilliant. Their acting is flawless. They both work at a diner, her as a waitress and him as a mysterious busboy. When she gets attacked on her way home one night, Adam is there to help fight the thugs. This is the beginning of their relationship. But not everyone is happy about the two of them being together, and Adam has not only a past, but also a health condition. Many people said this is a great romance movie and that they cried watching it.

Up Close and Personal (1996) PG-13

Some people have said that this is the best movie of all time. I loved this movie because of the great cast but it was also listed by a client as their cry movie. It's about a producer, Warren (Robert Redford), who hires a reporter, Tally (Michelle Pfeiffer). She rises to the rank of on-air personality and eventually gets promoted to a better job in a different city. Warren mentors her and their friendship turns into a heated relationship. There is a tragedy at the end that brings on the tears.

16

Injustice and Unfairness Movies

Watching someone suffer is difficult and emotional. These movies will bring out your empathic side.

Atonement (2007) R

> This is a movie about two people very much in love. Cecilia (Keira Knightley) and Robbie (James McAvoy) are torn apart by a lie told by Cecilia's jealous younger sister, Briony (Saoirse Ronan). Robbie is put in prison because of this lie and the consequences of Briony's lie affect them all. Then Cecilia and Robbie's paths cross when they meet again during World War II.

Gladiator (2000) R

> This movie is one of those rare epic movies that you will come back to time and time again. Maximus (Russell Crowe) gives an outstanding performance as a Roman general who is favored by the emperor, but the emperor's jealous son

(Joaquin Phoenix) kills his father and betrays Maximus by selling him into slavery and killing his wife and son. Maximus rises from a slave to become a champion gladiator who is more popular with the people than the evil emperor. Sworn to vindicate the deaths of his wife and son, Maximus is determined to take down the emperor. This is a great depiction of good vs evil.

Hotel Rwanda (2004) PG-13

Violent, unbelievable, and difficult to watch, this is an excellent movie about the horrors that happened to the Tutsi people in Rwanda, Africa in 1984. The Hutu military started a campaign to wipe out the entire Tutsi population. Hotel manager Paul Rusesabagina (Don Cheadle) bravely helps the refugees find shelter in his hotel. The U.N. pulls out and Paul finds himself alone in the struggle to protect these helpless people against the increasing violence by the Hutus. Very moving and sad to see how evil people can be when they turn against their own neighbors.

Introducing Dorothy Dandridge (1999) R

This true story is about the first African American woman to be nominated for an Oscar for Best Actress. Halle Berry plays Dorothy and gives a grand performance. What is difficult to watch is the way Dorothy is treated because of her race. Yet this beautiful woman carries on and becomes a star because of her determination and talent.

Like Dandelion Dust (2009) PG-13

This movie is taken from a novel written by Karen Kinsgbury, one of my favorite authors. It's a sad story about a precious little boy, Joey (Maxwell Perry Cotton), who has been adopted by loving parents, Jack (Cole Hauser) and Molly (Kate

Levering). But when Joey's biological father, Rip (Barry Pepper) is released from prison, he goes home and finds out that his wife, Wendy (Mira Sorvino), had given their baby up for adoption. He demands that they get the boy back, and though Wendy doesn't agree that this is the best thing for her son, she goes along with Rip. The authorities take the boy away from Jack and Molly, the only parents he has known, and put him in a home with an alcoholic abuser. If you've dealt with adoption in your life, this movie will tear you up. But watch to see what Wendy does in the end.

Mask (1985) PG-13

This is a true story about Rocky Dennis (Eric Stoltz), born with a facial deformity called "lionitis." He is outgoing, smart, and funny—but is ridiculed for the way he looks. His mom, Rusty (Cher), is his champion and, though she struggles with addiction, does her best to help her son be accepted in the school system. It's a sad but endearing movie that will touch your heart.

Patch Adams (1998) PG-13

This is a beautiful movie—a true story—about a man, Hunter "Patch" Adams (Robin Williams), who struggled with depression and spent time in a mental hospital. That experience propelled him to become a doctor so he could help other people. He used alternative methods and humor to help his patients. A wealthy friend helped him open a free clinic so he could help those who couldn't afford treatment. This movie touches the heart in so many ways.

Philadelphia (1993) PG-13

Tom Hanks won an Academy Award for his performance as Andrew Beckett, a successful lawyer for an impressive law firm. He had a secret—he was suffering from AIDS.

The law firm fired him for incompetence, but Andrew suspected it was because he was homosexual and had AIDS. Andrew decided to sue them for wrongful termination. He had trouble finding someone to take his case until he met Joe Miller (Denzel Washington) who, homophobic though he was, finally agreed to take his case. Mary Steenburgen is the attorney fighting against Andrew's lawsuit.

The Book Thief (2013) PG-13

Watch the trailer of this movie and you will want to see what it's about. A young girl without hope, Liesel (Sophie Nelisse), is adopted by a German couple (Geoffrey Rush and Emily Watson). She doesn't know how to read, so her new dad teaches her. Soon, they must help hide a Jew (Ben Schnetzer) from the Nazis. In this scary world she finds herself in, Liesel discovers the beauty of words and imagination through books as she copes with the events happening in her town. Heartbreaking, yet heartwarming. I've been told that the book is even sadder than the movie.

The Color Purple (1985) PG-13

When I was in my late twenties and single, I went to see this movie in the theater with a bunch of friends, mostly guys. The one thing I remember is that as soon as the movie ended, the lights came on way too soon. I immediately put my head in my lap so I could hide the fact that I was crying my eyes out. I made everyone wait until I could regain my composure. This was a great movie and so very sad. I've never watched it since, but even so, I still remember the love between these sisters who lived worlds apart. This movie stars Whoopi Goldberg as Celie, Oprah Winfrey as Sofia, and Danny Glover as Albert. It spans the life of Celie over forty years and, though difficult to watch because of all the abuse, it has a tender heartwarming ending.

The Elephant Man (1980) PG

This is another one of those movies that will leave you in tears if you have a heart. The personal tragedy of John Merrick (John Hurt), who was born with a congenital disorder that left him horribly disfigured, was that he was rejected and ridiculed all his life. He was labeled "The Elephant Man" and was featured in a freak show. Dr. Frederic Treves (Anthony Hopkins) found him and brought him home and learned what a kind and gentle soul he was, despite the way others treated him all his life.

The Green Mile (1999) R

I saw this movie years ago and had no idea, until researching movies that were recommended to me, that it was written by Stephen King. It is an excellent movie. John Coffey (Michael Clarke Duncan) is on death row. Paul Edgecomb (Tom Hanks) is the officer who will walk the green mile with him. It was called the green mile because the floor was covered with green linoleum, which prisoners walking to their execution walked on. Even though this is a three-hour movie, it is captivating to watch, with excellent performances by Hanks and Duncan.

To Kill a Mockingbird (1962) NR

This movie is a great one to watch. It stars Gregory Peck as Atticus Finch, a small-town lawyer and widower raising two children on his own: Scout (Mary Badham) and Jem (Phillip Alford). Atticus defends a black man, Tom Robinson (Brock Peters) against false rape charges and trouble ensues. His children get a first-hand view of the evils of racism and stereotyping.

17

Love of Animal Movies

When you have had the privilege to love an animal, you will experience deep emotions when you watch a movie dealing with animals, especially if there is any mistreatment or loss of an animal.

Babe (1995) G

> What's not to like about this movie? You will cry both sad and happy tears while watching it. I still say "That'll do, pig" when someone does something correctly, but I always must explain because they think I am calling them a pig. Arthur Hoggett is a farmer who wins a pig, Babe (Christine Cavanaugh), at a county fair. He plans to fatten it up to serve it for Christmas dinner but finds that Babe is no ordinary pig. Adopted by the motherly border collie, Fly (Miriam Margolyes), Babe learns that he can herd sheep. Guaranteed to entertain you and bring a few tears, this is one movie to add to your watch list.

Bambi (1942) G

Bambi is every child's first experience in cry movies. Unless you've never seen it, you'll never understand why hunting deer is offensive to us because deer hunters killed Bambi's mother. The movie starts with a young Bambi exploring his world. He makes friends with Thumper the rabbit, and Flower the skunk. He has a doting mother who teaches him that he shouldn't go in the open meadow because there are hunters there. His father is The Great Prince of the Forest. As Bambi grows up, he learns the valuable lesson that life has tragedy and beauty in his forest home.

Because of Winn Dixie (2005) PG

Opal (AnnaSophia Robb) is a ten-year-old girl who just moved to a small town in Florida with her preacher father (Jeff Daniels). Opal, having been abandoned by her mother years before, is lonely and misses her old friends. She discovers a cute and active little dog that she names Winn-Dixie because she found him in the Winn Dixie store. Her new four-legged friend helps her make new friends and repair her relationship with her father.

Black Beauty (1994) G

This is one of my top three cry movies. Just watching the opening credits makes me cry. I love animals and cannot stand to see them suffer. Horses, though majestic, are easily controlled and often abused. Black Beauty is no exception. Told from the perspective of the horse, Black Beauty has a relaxed life in the English countryside with his mother but is sold to new owners and his life takes a downward turn. He has some good owners throughout his life, but still suffers hardships. The good news is that this movie has a great ending which will have you sobbing, if you love horses as much as I do.

Charlotte's Web (2006) G

This film is endearing to young children and children-at-heart. The animals are all friends, and when a spider named Charlotte (Julia Roberts) learns that her friend, Wilbur the pig (Dominic Scott Kay), is going to be killed, she takes action. Fern (Dakota Fanning) is the little girl who befriends Wilbur.

Hachi: A Dog's Tale (2009) G

This movie is lighthearted and fun to watch but will tear your heart out at the end. It's a true story of a man named Parker (Richard Gere) who befriends a dog he finds (Hachi). This story shows why dogs are known as Man's Best Friend. Parker and Hachi form a special bond. But when something happens to Parker, watch what Hachi does.

Marley And Me (2008) PG

I did my best not to cry in this movie. I started off thinking how much I hated this dog. But my resolve didn't last. I sobbed my eyes out at this movie. John and Jenny Grogan (Owen Wilson & Jennifer Aniston) move to Florida and adopt Marley into their family. Marly fails obedience school and basically destroys everything he comes in contact with, but he is still loveable. This is a good movie that starts you off crying about the dog, but leaves you crying about other things in your heart that need grieving over.

My Dog Skip (2000) PG

What a wonderful movie! I wanted to buy a Jack Russell Terrier after watching this movie, but with three dogs already, my husband and I decided against it. Willie Morris (Frankie Muniz) always wanted a dog, but his dad, Jack (Kevin Bacon), didn't think he needed one. When mom Ellen (Diane Lane) surprised Willie with a puppy on his birthday, Jack refused to let him keep it. Hooray for mom, because she put her foot down on this one and Willie got to keep Skip, who became his best friend. Skip helps Willie make new friends, and bond with unlikely people, including the most beautiful girl in his school. You will laugh and cry as you watch this. This movie will stay with you for a very long time.

Old Yeller (1957) G

Who doesn't know what this movie is about? Even though it came out the year before I was born, it was the first movie I ever remember being traumatized by as a small child. Travis (Tommy Kirk) is left with his mom Katie (Dorothy McGuire) and his brother Arliss (Kevin Corcoran) while their dad and husband, Jim (Fess Parker) is away on a cattle drive. A runaway dog named Old Yeller damages one of their fields and they try to run him off. But after he saves Arliss from a bear attack, they decide to keep him. Travis and the faithful Old Yeller form a bond until an outbreak of rabies strikes. Grab the box of tissues. You will need it.

The Land Before Time (1988) G

This may be an animated movie for children, but it has some sad parts to it. This is also one of my daughter's cry movies because she has always loved dinosaurs and she watched this movie many times growing up. The main character, Littlefoot, learns some hard lessons about life, along with his friends, Petrie, Ducky, Spike & Cera. Both you and your children will be touched by this movie.

Where The Red Fern Grows (1974) G

The first time I saw this movie was with my husband and kids at home. My daughter was seven and my son was four.

Of course, I was crying through some of it. My daughter was looking at me and at the movie. I think she didn't know why I was crying. I didn't want her watching me cry, so I went and sat in front of them on the floor to finish it out. As it ended, I turned around and saw my four-year-old son with huge tears streaming down his face. He has had a thing for dogs ever since. This is a wonderful movie about a boy, Billy (Stewart Peterson), who really wants some coon dogs because he wants to hunt raccoons. He finally saves up money and buys two dogs, Dan and Ann. He trains them to be prizewinning hunters. Watch until the end to find out why the movie has its name. If you didn't cry before this, you will at the end. Throughout the movie, you will have both sad and happy tears.

White Fang (1991) PG

Another tearjerker of a movie, this one has a happy ending. It's about a man named Jack (Ethan Hawke), who travels to Alaska to find his deceased father's mining camp. Jack finds a dog/wolf hybrid, White Fang, who is being abused by his owner by being made to fight a fierce bulldog. Injured and dying, Jack rescues him, brings him back to his camp, and nurses him back to health. Though trained to be vicious and territorial, Jack tames White Fang, and they form a strong bond. Beautiful scenic views of Alaska are a bonus.

18

Power of Love Movies

Seeing love triumph and conquer can often bring us to tears. Love of family and love of friends is a very powerful emotion.

Imitation of Life (1959) NR

This is probably the toughest movie to watch. It is on the list of my top three favorite cry movies. There is an earlier version (1934) but this one is my favorite. Lana Turner is Lora, an aspiring actress who is single with a small daughter, Suzie (Sandra Dee). She encounters Annie (Juanita Moore), mother of Sarah Jane (Susan Kohner), at the beach as the two mothers are desperately searching for their daughters. They find them playing together. Annie is an African American widow, but Sarah Jane has light skin and looks Caucasian. Lora takes them in to live with her since they have nowhere to go, and they end up forming a close bond. Annie takes care of Suzie (also cooks and cleans) while Lora looks for work as an actress. The girls enjoy playing together. Trouble starts when Annie brings Sarah Jane an umbrella to school on a rainy day. The teacher tells Annie that there are no "colored" children in her class. When Annie points to Sarah Jane and says that she is her daughter, Sarah Jane runs out the room and tells her mother she hates her. The entire movie is a great depiction of a mother's unconditional love for her daughter, who rejects her all her life. Lora does end up becoming a famous actress, but Annie's heart is broken because of the rejection of her daughter. This is such a great movie, but so sad to watch.

On Golden Pond (1981) PG

This is an excellent movie that addresses the difficult subject of aging parents. Norman and Ethel Thayer (Henry Fonda and Katharine Hepburn) spend their summers in New England at their vacation home on Golden Pond. This year, their daughter, Chelsea (Jane Fonda) comes to visit with her fiancé, Bill Ray (Dabney Coleman), and his son, Billy (Doug McKeon). Chelsea and Bill leave for a trip to Europe but leave Billy with her parents. Old, cantankerous Norman is difficult to live with, but Billy soon begins to bond with Norman. Chelsea finally returns and attempts to build back her strained relationship with her father. Touching, especially since Henry and Jane are a real father/daughter pair who have had basically the same relationship as the one depicted here. I believe this was Henry's last movie, as he died a year after making this movie.

The Five People You Meet in Heaven (2004) NR

This movie stars one of my favorite actors (Jon Voight) as Eddie, an aging handyman who works at a carnival. As Eddie is attempting to save a small child from death, he himself dies. He goes to heaven and is met by five people who had an impact on his life. Each one of these five people recreates a crucial event from his life on earth to help Eddie answer his life's most troubling question and explain some of the tragedies he encountered. A tearjerker, but well written and acted.

The Iron Giant (1999) PG

I saw this animated movie in the theater when my daughter was nine. I remember crying because of the sad, misunderstood giant robot (Vin Diesel), who befriends a little boy, Hogarth (Eli Marienthal). However, the government soon learns of the robot and is determined to exterminate him. Hogarth must show that the Iron Giant is harmless and safe. With voices by Harry Connick, Jr., Jennifer Aniston, and John Mahoney, this is a cute film with sad undertones. It will touch the heart of those individuals who feel misunderstood.

The Story of Us (1999) R

This is a movie I have recommended to many married couples, showing them that the grass isn't always greener on the other side. I won't give away the ending, but believe me, it's well worth the watch. Katie (Michelle Pfeiffer) and Ben (Bruce Willis) have been married for fifteen years with two kids. At the beginning of the summer, they send their kids off to camp and they plan to have a trial separation to see if they should split up for good. The plan is to let their kids know their decision at the end of the summer when they pick them up. In the meantime, they both start dating other people, but woven throughout this are flashbacks of their heated love life and volatile outbursts. I love the scene where they are having an argument in bed, and you see both sets of parents show up (not in reality) to feed into their arguments. This movie has funny and sad parts in it, but the final scene is the takeaway that I love.

19

Sacrifice Movies

Movies that depict human sacrifices, especially for the good of others, cause deep emotions in most people.

Armageddon (1998) PG-13

Harry Stamper (Bruce Willis) is a famous oil driller, known for his ability to tackle dangerous and difficult projects. When NASA bigwig Dan Truman (Billy Bob Thornton) discovers that an asteroid is soon to collide with Earth, he approaches Harry to do the job to stop it. Harry insists on bringing his own crew with him. Among his crew members is A.J. (Ben Affleck) who is dating Harry's daughter, Grace (Liv Tyler), against Harry's wishes. The crew lands on the asteroid and plants an atomic bomb that will blow it up and save the Earth. But the unexpected happens and someone must stay behind to detonate the bomb.

Braveheart (1995) R

This movie is loosely based on William Wallace's (Mel Gibson) life in Scotland as a medieval Scottish warrior, who is driven to revenge when his wife is slaughtered. This is not a movie for the fainthearted, but this is a popular pick of a cry movie for men. The torture of William at the end was a bit too much for me, but William proved to be a valiant warrior to the end.

Glory (1989) R

This is a true story about the first all-African American regiment during the American Civil War. Led by Col. Robert Gould Shaw (Matthew Broderick), this strong unit of soldiers goes from doing menial and unimportant tasks, to being recognized as worthy to be placed in the heat of the battle. With an all-star cast including Denzel Washington and Morgan Freeman, this is an excellent movie that has a bittersweet end. Because of what these men did and the bravery they showed, the US began to accept thousands of African American men for combat.

Schindler's List (1993) R

Winner of seven Academy Awards including Best Picture and Best Director (Steven Spielberg), this movie is probably one of the most historically significant movies of all time. This true story takes place in Germany where a German man, Oskar Schindler (Liam Neeson), opens a factory in Germany and staffs it with Jewish workers. When the SS begins exterminating Jewish people, Schindler does what he can to protect his workers so his factory can stay in operation. In doing so, he also saves innocent lives of the Jews. He saved more that 1,100 Jews during the Holocaust. This is a sad movie to watch, but inspiring to see what one person can do to save humanity.

The Last of The Mohicans (1992) R

This is a violent, but romantic movie during the French and Indian War. Hawkeye (Daniel Day-Lewis) is the half-white brother of Incas (Eric Schweig) from the Mohican tribe. Cora (Madeleine Stowe) is the daughter of a British colonel who is kidnapped with her sister, Alice (Jodhi May), by a traitor scout. Hawkeye and his brother set out to rescue them as they continue to fight in the war effort. Described as masterful, this movie has been listed as an adult male's cry movie.

The Passion of The Christ (2004) R

This is an excellent movie directed by Mel Gibson. The life of Jesus Christ is documented and it's difficult to watch how brutally this Man of God was treated by His own people. I had to step out of the theater during the crucifixion because I couldn't watch it. It will cause you to weep when you realize the sacrifice this Man made for all people. I hope it will draw you closer to Him when you see how much He loves everyone. Jim Caviezel does an excellent job portraying Jesus Christ.

The Song of Bernadette (1943) NR

This is one of my mother's favorite cry movies, which is a true story that took place in 1858. A young French girl, Bernadette Soubirous (Jennifer Jones), begins to experience visions of the Virgin Mary. At first no one believes her, and they think she has gone mad. However, her priest, Dominique Peyramale (Charles Bickford), begins to believe her. Bernadette is eventually deemed a saint and she becomes a nun. This is a beautiful depiction of a faithful and humble woman. Many have commented that they wept as they watched this movie.

20

Tragedy and Trauma Movies

It's tough to see someone get hurt or upset by something outside of their control. Our ability to empathize provokes our tears.

About Schmidt (2002) R

> Warren Schmidt (Jack Nicholson) retires from selling insurance and finds that he is not happy with his marriage of forty years. When his wife, Helen, dies suddenly of a brain aneurysm, Warren finds himself incredibly lonely. He also discovers that his best friend Ray had an affair with Helen because he found love letters in her closet. Lonely and distraught with no direction in his life, he sets out in his Winnebago and travels to Colorado to visit his daughter and her fiancé—hoping to split the couple up. Warren ends up attending the wedding, then heads home feeling lost and alone. Any movie starring Jack Nicholson will be entertaining, but this movie deals with the sad reality of being alone and lonely in your old age. Warren realizes that he must make the most of what life he has left.

Angela's Ashes (1999) R

This movie is set in the 1930s during the depression. The McCourt family decides to travel from America to Ireland. They are poverty stricken and struggle not only with deaths and money troubles, but the father, Malachy Sr. (Robert Carlyle), is an unemployable alcoholic. This is a powerful movie depicting the challenges and continual problems they must face. The oldest son, Frank (Michael Legge), wrote this memoir of his family's travails as he was growing up. It's a tragic but poignant story.

Good Will Hunting (1997) R

Let me caution you about this movie. The language may disturb you. F-bombs throughout, which fits well with the character. But if you do your best to ignore those, this is a great story of Will Hunting (Matt Damon), who has a genius level IQ but is working as a janitor. He suffered severe child abuse and, through counseling, gradually puts his life back in order with the help of therapist Sean Maguire (Robin Williams). I loved this movie, because it shows the struggles we go through when we've had a horrible childhood. But it gives hope that things can get better.

Jack (1996) PG-13

This is such a cute, but bittersweet movie. Karen Powell (Diane Lane) is the mother of Jack (Robin Williams), who was born with a rare condition that causes his body to age much faster than normal. Little ten-year-old Jack looks like he's forty but is emotionally still a kid. Jack's big personality helps him make friends, which gives him a richer life. Any movie with Robin Williams in it is going to be entertaining and this one surely delivers.

Legends Of the Fall (1994) R

The reviews for this movie are outstanding. It is a beautiful movie, with passion, conflict, family betrayal, and violence. And, of course, a stellar cast. Colonel William Ludlow (Anthony Hopkins), moved to the Montana wilderness after becoming disillusioned with the Army's treatment of the Indians. He has three sons, Alfred (Aidan Quinn), Tristan (Brad Pitt), and Samuel (Henry Thomas). Susanna (Julia Ormond) starts out as Samuel's fiancée, but he leaves to fight in WWI before they marry. He gets killed, and both Tristan and Alfred fall for her. Lots of heartache and sorrow. Your heart strings will be pulled watching this epic movie.

Les Misérables (2002) PG-13

This is an epic French period musical film that features Hugh Jackman as Jean Valjean, a man who was imprisoned for nineteen years for stealing bread for his nephew. He is freed by Javert (Russell Crowe), who is responsible for the prison's workforce. However, Valjean has trouble finding work. He is sheltered by a kind bishop, but Valjean steals his silver and is caught by the police. The bishop tells police he gave the silver to Valjean, and he encourages Valjean to use the silver to start an honest life. Valjean breaks parole and reinvents himself as a mayor and a factory owner. Eight years later, Valjean helps a dying worker, Fantine (Anne Hathaway), by agreeing to care for her daughter, Cosette (Amanda Seyfried). But Valjean hasn't escaped from Javert, who continues to look for him all these years later. This is a great movie, but there are several sad parts to get your tears flowing.

Life Is Beautiful (1997) PG-13

This movie won three Academy Awards: Best Foreign Film, Best Actor, and Best Musical Score. It is such an uplifting movie. Guido (Roberto Benigni) meets and charms Dora (Nicolette Braschi) into marrying him. They have a son, Giosue (Girogio Cantarini) and they live an idyllic life. But tragedy happens when Guido and Giosue are taken to a concentration camp, and they are separated from Dora. It's heartwarming to see how hard Guido tries to show Giosue that all is well by trying to pretend it's all just a game. Guido is a wonderful example of a husband and father. The ending will break your heart.

Me Before You (2016) PG-13

What a wonderful movie this is! I want to watch it again as I'm describing it here. This movie basically defines love in its purest form. Innocent and free-spirited Louisa "Lou" (Emilia Clark) can't seem to hold down a job and rejects the prospect of most jobs offered to her. That is, until she accepts a job as caregiver to Will Traynor (Sam Claflin), a wealthy young banker who becomes paralyzed after being hit by a motorcycle. Poor Will is depressed and has no desire to do anything except complain. When he meets Lou, he initially rejects her, but she slowly works her magic and wins him over. Their experiences will warm your heart—but grab the tissues for the ending.

Mrs. Miniver (1942) NR

This Academy Award winning movie has an excellent cast (for those of you old enough to remember these actors). Filmed in black and white, the movie depicts the struggles of a middle-class English family living through World War II. It won awards for Best Picture, Best Director, Best Script,

Best Supporting Actress, and Best Actress. Greer Garson is Madame Curie, wife of Clem (Walter Pidgeon). The movie also stars Teresa Wright and Henry Travers. This is an inspiring film filled with hope, love, heartache, and bravery. You will be glad you watched this one.

One Flew Over the Cuckoo's Nest (1975) R

This is a classic movie that has always been difficult for me to watch because of the treatment these patients receive. Jack Nicholson gives his best performance as a mental health patient who endures abusive treatment at the hands of Nurse Ratched (Louise Fletcher). It won all five major Academy Awards (Best Picture, Best Actor in a Lead Role, Best Actress in a Lead Role, Best Director, and Best Screenplay). Randle McMurphy (Jack Nicholson) is sent to a mental institution for evaluation from a prison. But he and cruel Nurse Ratched get into battles time and time again because she determines that the rebellious Randle is a threat to her authority. She is inflexible and he is irreverent and feisty. The movie also stars Danny DeVito and Christopher Lloyd.

Radio (2003) PG

Here is yet another one of my favorite movies. This is a heartwarming true story about a twenty-three-year-old mentally disabled man named Radio (Cuba Gooding, Jr.), who is befriended by the high school coach Jones (Ed Harris). Radio lives alone with his mother, who is a nurse. Because she is gone most days, Radio wanders around the town pushing a shopping cart and picking up odds and ends that he finds. He has such as sweet soul but is bullied by some football players when Coach Jones steps in to rescue him. This movie has some extremely sad parts and some extremely joyful parts. You will not be disappointed with the performances and the emotions running through this movie.

Romeo and Juliet (1968) PG-13

Most people know what this tragic love story is about. It's one of William Shakespeare's best love stories. There have been two more recent movies made, but my favorite is the 1968 version. There is a long-time feud between the Capulet family and the Montague family. When Juliet (Olivia Hussey), a Capulet, falls in love with Romeo (Leonard Whiting), a Montague, they decide to elope. This creates even more tension between the families. They devise a brilliant plan to be together—or so they think.

Saving Private Ryan (1998) R

This is a great movie directed by Steven Spielberg about the search for a man whose three brothers were killed in combat. The mission is to bring the last brother home safely. The all-star cast includes, Tom Hanks, Matt Damon, Tom Sizemore, Vin Diesel, Edward Burns and Barry Pepper. This movie shows that war is hell and the men fighting in the war are courageous and honorable.

Shawshank Redemption (1994) R

Sometimes, just looking at who stars in a movie can determine if you'd like to watch it. Morgan Freeman is one of those actors. When I see his name listed in the cast, I know it's going to be good. This movie does not disappoint. It is about the brutality of prison life, and the irrepressible emotion of hope. Andy Dufresne (Tim Robbins) is sentenced to two consecutive life sentences in prison for murdering his wife and her lover (yet he is innocent). While in prison, he forms a friendship with Red (Morgan Freeman). Over the next twenty years, the two friends form a close bond. I have heard from so many people this this is their favorite movie of all time. Definitely worth the watch.

Silence Of the Heart (1984) NR

I added this movie to this book because a dear client of mine named Mark, said this was his cry movie because it broke him up when he heard that the father in this movie admitted that he loved his son (after his son's suicide). Mark came from an abusive home with a father who never loved him. This made-for-tv-movie is difficult to locate, but it is about a high school senior, Skip (Chad Lowe), who discovers that he didn't pass his college entrance exam and may have to go to community college. He is also in love with a girl in his class who doesn't give him the time of day. He decides to commit suicide by driving his car off a cliff because he can't face disappointing his father and feels misunderstood by everyone. His best friend, Ken (Charlie Sheen) struggles with the guilt he has because Skip told him he was going to kill himself, but Ken didn't believe him. It's a sad story to watch as you discover how suicide affects so many people.

Sophie's Choice (1982) R

Meryl Streep has always been one of my favorite actresses because of her talent. She is excellent in this hard-to-watch movie. Sophie (Meryl Streep) is a holocaust survivor with a terrible secret. Now living in Brooklyn in 1947, she and her lover Nathan (Kevin Kline), make friends with a tenant in their building named Stingo (Peter MacNicol). Sophie has flashbacks that unravel her harrowing story in Auschwitz. Stingo grows close to Sophie and wants to save her, but only Nathan can ease her pain. There is so much depth to this movie. It is awful (to hear about what Sophie went through), yet at the same time it is endearing (she finally finds her peace).

The Boy in The Striped Pajamas (2008) PG-13

This is such a good movie! It shows the innocence of children and how much wiser they can be than the adults in their lives. An eight-year-old boy named Bruno (Asa Butterfield) must leave his friends in Berlin because his dad has just accepted a job as a commandant in Hitler's army. They live near a concentration camp where his father (David Thewlis) will be working. Upset and without friends in this new place, he wanders around the property and happens upon a Jewish boy his own age behind a barbed-wire-fence that separates his property from the camp. They become friends with no idea that they are supposed to be enemies. This is a poignant film, with an ending that will totally gut you.

The Fault in Our Stars (2014) PG-13

This very touching and emotional movie is about a girl named Hazel Grace Lancaster (Shailene Woodley), who is only sixteen years old yet has cancer. She feels hopeless about her illness, but she is encouraged by her mom and dad to go to a cancer support group. There, she meets Gus Waters (Ansel Elgort), who is also a cancer patient in remission. He pressures her to become his friend and she reluctantly does, describing herself as a grenade, about to blow up. But they fall in love and help each other find meaning in their lives.

The Last Samurai (2003) R

Tom Cruise plays Capt. Nathan Algren, an American military officer who gets hired by the Emperor of Japan to train the Japanese army in the art of modern warfare. The Japanese government wants to eradicate the ancient Samurai warrior class. In a battle he wasn't totally prepared for against the Samurai, Capt. Algren gets taken prisoner by the Samurai leader Katsumoto, and lives in the village among his family.

Algren eventually gains the respect of Kasumoto, and they become friends. Alden saves his life when some ninja's infiltrate their village. Tom Cruise and Ken Watanabe are excellent in this film. It's a great movie to see.

The Phantom of The Opera (2004) PG-13

The main thing I remember about this movie is that my daughter was obsessed with it after she saw it when she was fourteen. The music is still playing in my mind as I'm writing this. It's a sad and tragic love story with excellent acting and soulful, beautiful music. The Phantom (Gerard Butler) lives underneath a nineteenth century opera house in Paris. He is fascinated with the beautiful singer, Christine (Emmy Rossum). The Phantom works behind the scenes with management to get Christine the key roles so he can keep her nearby. Unaware of this, Christine falls for her childhood friend, Raoul (Patrick Wilson) instead. In fear of losing Christine and wanting to keep her near, the Phantom develops a scheme that Raoul tries to stop. Keep the tissues nearby for this movie.

The Pianist (2002) R

Winner of three Academy Awards, including Best Actor, this is an extraordinary movie. It is the true story of Wladyslaw Szpilman (Adrien Brody), an accomplished pianist who plays on the Polish radio during World War II. He survived in Warsaw by hiding in various locations among the ruins. He gets separated from his family and barely has food to eat. Starving and jaundiced, he is discovered by a German officer, Wilm Hosenfeld (Thomas Kretschmann), who discovers that he is a pianist and asks him to play. Hosenfeld lets him hide in the attic of the empty house and regularly supplies him with food. Hosenfeld is later captured and put in a Soviet prisoner-of-war camp for German soldiers. After the war ends, Szpilman is back playing on Polish radio.

The Pride of The Yankees (1942) NR

Nominated for eleven Academy Awards, this true story is about the life of baseball great Lou Gehrig (Gary Cooper). Lou played for the New York Yankees and played alongside Babe Ruth, to make the Yankees the team to beat. Gehrig meets and marries Eleanor (Teresa Wright), and his career takes off. He is the crowd favorite. But one day he notices that his strength is declining. After a few more games, he benches himself and is taken to the doctor, only to learn of his incurable disease. This is a tearjerker for sure, especially when he gives his farewell speech at the end.

The Prince of Tides (1991) R

Tom Wingo (Nick Nolte), a teacher and football coach, is asked by his mom to fly to New York to talk to his twin sister, Savannah's (Melinda Dillon) psychiatrist after yet another suicide attempt by her. In so doing, Nick not only develops a relationship with this psychiatrist, Susan Lowenstein (Barbra Streisand), but also unearths a traumatic memory he had at age thirteen that he had kept hidden. I'll never forget the male client who told me why this was his cry movie. It was the tragedy that Tom endured that brought up my client's own issues regarding this type of trauma. He was able to have his catharsis by watching this movie.

Titanic (1997) PG-13

This movie depicts the disaster of the maiden voyage of the RMS Titanic in 1912, the largest moving object ever built. It chronicles the romance of Rose Dewitt (Kate Winslet), who is engaged to be married to a wealthy man, Cal Hockley (Billy Zane)—a man who can help resolve her family's financial problems. She plans to throw herself overboard because she doesn't want to marry Cal. However, Jack Dawson

(Leonardo DiCaprio) discovers her plan and stops her before she jumps off the ship. Jack is a starving artist who won a ticket aboard the boat in a card game. They develop a torrid relationship on board the ill-fated ship.

Unbroken (2014) PG-13

Another true story, this movie is about Louis "Louis" Zamperini (Jack O'Connell). Once a troubled kid, his older brother encourages him to turn his life around and he ends up becoming a runner who was so fast, he qualified for the 1936 Olympics. When World War II begins, he joins the military, but his plane crashes in the Pacific and he survives with two other crewmen for forty-seven days in a raft. The Japanese Navy captures the men and takes them to a POW camp, where Louie is targeted by the cruel prison commander and is brutally abused. This movie is difficult to watch, but what stands out is the incredible power of the human spirit.

United 93 (2006) R

This is a tragic film about United Flight 93, the fourth hijacked plane on 9/11, and what the passengers did to stop the terrorists from succeeding in their mission to blow up the U.S. Capitol.

We Were Soldiers (2002) R

With an all-star cast, including Mel Gibson, Sam Elliott, Greg Kinnear, and Madeline Stowe, this is an excellent depiction of what the war was like during the battle between the US and North Vietnam. Violent and sad, we see uncommon valor and bravery under fire, along with loyalty among the solders. I didn't see this movie, but it was listed as a male client's cry movie.

21

Triumph Movies

We love to watch someone rise to greatness. Our tears are usually happy tears. Once the tears begin, it's easy to let the emotions bubble up from other issues we may be feeling.

Cinderella Man (2005) PG-13

> This is a rags-to-riches true story of a day laborer, Jim Braddock (Russell Crowe), who struggles to find work during the Great Depression. His wife, Mae (Renee Zellweger) is a strong supporter of her husband. But when he gets an opportunity to return to boxing against a favored contender, Mae worries that he will get seriously hurt. He wins that fight much to the delight of the entire town. But he sets his sights on an even bigger fight—against the defending champion, Max Baer. This movie was directed by Ron Howard, who does an excellent job. Great movie.

Million Dollar Baby (2004) PG-13

This movie is about a fighter wannabee named Maggie Fitzgerald (Hilary Swank), who shows up at Frankie Dunn's (Clint Eastwood) gym asking if he would train her. He tells her he doesn't train girls, but Maggie is relentless and shows up every day to practice. Finally, Frankie agrees to be her trainer. Frankie and Maggie work well together and she starts winning. They develop a tight bond, realizing that they only have each other as support. The ending is very sad, but the story still inspires.

Rocky (1976) PG

This is a great movie, winning Best Picture at the Academy Awards in 1976. Rocky Balboa (Sylvester Stallone) is a working-class American who is uneducated but dreams of becoming a world class boxer. His best friend, Paulie (Burt Young), helps Rocky get a date with his sister Adrian (Talia Shire), and the two fall in love. Rocky gets a chance to fight Apollo Creed, the current heavyweight boxing world champion, who selects Rocky as the local contender to fight him. Rocky has no confidence that he will win the fight—he just wants to go the distance in the ring with him. This is an uplifting and inspirational movie. There were eight sequels to this first movie, which speaks of its popularity.

Rudy (1993) PG

This is the most popular sports film that guys have said was their cry movie. It's a true story of Daniel "Rudy" Ruettiger who grew up wanting to play football for the University of Notre Dame, but his prospects were grim—he didn't have the grades or the funds to be able to attend. Through sheer determination and persistence, and with the help of friends along the way, Rudy is admitted to Notre Dame his senior year and works his way onto the football team. This movie has such a happy ending that you will be crying when you see it. Very touching and inspirational.

Southpaw (2015) R

This is a bittersweet movie about a junior middleweight boxing champion, Billy "The Great" Hope (Jake Gyllenhaal), who has a loving wife, Maureen (Rachel McAdams), and daughter Leila (Oona Laurence). Billy has a promising career ahead of him, but a tragedy happens that unravels his life. He loses his family, his house, and his manager. He eventually meets trainer Tick Willis (Forest Whitaker) who reluctantly agrees to train him. Billy works hard to get back in shape and repair broken relationships.

The Goodbye Girl (1977) PG

This is one of my all-time favorite triumph movies. Any movie written by Neil Simon is guaranteed to be a winner. The theme song is sung by the lead singer (David Gates) of my favorite band, Bread, even though I believe that David had gone solo when this song came out. The movie is about a struggling dancer named Paula (Marsha Mason), doing her best to raise her daughter Lucy (Quinn Cummings) in New York. One evening, Paula is awakened by a persistent knock on her door, only to find Elliot Garfield (Richard Dreyfuss) standing there with proof that he now owns the lease on this apartment. Paula's former boyfriend sub-let her apartment unbeknownst to her and she is furious. She and Elliott reach an agreement for all three to live there, but they do not get along. Gradually, they warm up to each other and sparks soon fly. You will laugh quite a bit as you watch this movie, and the end will cause you to cry happy tears.

The Natural (1984) PG

Great baseball movie about Roy Hobbs (Robert Redford), who travels to Chicago to try out with the Chicago Cubs. But before he can try out, he meets an unstable girl named Harriet, who invites him to her room and shoots him in the stomach then kills herself. The story picks up sixteen years later when Roy is signed as a rookie for the New York Knights, the last-place team. With Roy on board, the Knights start winning. This is an exciting, inspirational movie with a few twists thrown in. A moving performance by Robert Redford and Glenn Close, as Iris.

Index

Bibliography

American Standard Version Bible, BibleGateway.com.

Bergman, Jerry. "The Miracle of Tears." Creation, September, 1993, pages 16-18.

Biebel, D. B., Dill, J. E., and Dill, B. (2008). *The A to Z Guide to Healthier Living.* Revell.

Frey, W.H. (1977). *Crying: The Mystery of Tears.* Texas: Winston Press.

Gray, H. (1959). "Anatomy of the Human Body." Glo Bible, 27th ed., pages 1121, 1122.

Levoy, Gregg. "Tears That Speak." Psychology Today, July/August, 1988, pages 8-10.

Mason, Ruth. "Why You Should Let Kids Cry." Parents, December, 1995, pages 65-66.

Reardon, Patrick. "For Crying Out Loud." Houston Chronicle, April 3, 2000, Page 1C, 10C.

Rees, W. Dewi. "Bereavement and Illness." Journal of Thanatology 2, Summer-Fall, 1972, pages 814-819.

Parachin, V. M. "Have a Good Cry." http://www.cyquest.com/good_cry.html.

About the Author

Sally Scott Creed is a native of Lafayette, Louisiana. She has been an LPC for thirty years and has a private practice in Lafayette. She had a private practice in the Houston area for sixteen years before moving back home to Lafayette. She maintains her Texas license and continues to see online clients who live in Texas. Though Sally has written articles for three years in a local magazine, this is her first published book. She has two grown  children: Courtney, who lives in North Carolina, and Adam, who lives in Texas. Sally is married to Don, who has been her encouragement to finish this book, and they have two amazing dogs named Boomer and Cooper. When she's not working, Sally enjoys gardening, reading and knitting. If you'd like to contact Sally, to add your cry movie to her list, or for comments or questions, send her an email at cryingbook22@gmail.com.

Printed in the United States
by Baker & Taylor Publisher Services